More Praise for *The Right-Brain Busin*

"Like to know how to get paid to do work you love th
this book. It's an imaginative way to visually map out
you can see what you need to do. Keeping your goals ...
mind will keep them top-of-mind. Read it and reap."
— SAM HORN, The Intrigue Expert and author of *POP!*

"Who doesn't procrastinate just thinking about planning? Crack through
your resistance and get your business rolling by following Jennifer Lee's
great tips for engaging your imagination and your intuition."
— ERIC MAISEL, author of *Mastering Creative Anxiety*

"Jennifer Lee successfully captures the energy, creativity, and passion that
go into starting your own business. The advice she gives through both
illustrations and text help make the dream of hanging your own shin-
gle very real and very exciting."
— CAITLIN FRIEDMAN, coauthor of
The Girl's Guide to Starting Your Own Business

"Creatively smart and inspiringly intelligent, *The Right-Brain Business
Plan* is a must-read for any entrepreneur who wants to tap into the
power of both sides of their brain. You'll jump with enthusiasm into
the parts of your business you have avoided for far too long!"
— CHRISTINE ARYLO, MBA turned inspirational catalyst
and author of *Choosing ME before WE*

"Creatives, unite! Finally, there's a way you can be gloriously you — and
have a plan you love to work from. Move over, spreadsheets — this is
business planning for the rest of us."
— ANDREA J. LEE, CEO of The Wealthy Thought Leader

"This is one of those rare books I cannot wait to mark up, get paint on,
and really use (vs. those that stay on the shelf intimidating me). If you
yearn to do your own thing but believe you can't because you're too
creative or intuitive or disorganized or whatever, stop that voice in your

head right now and listen to Jennifer Lee's funky, delightful, seasoned help instead. If I did it, and all the people Jennifer has helped did it, you can, too."

— JENNIFER LOUDEN, author of *The Life Organizer*

"*The Right-Brain Business Plan* provides a framework for the creative entrepreneur who needs a nudge in the right direction with easy-to-follow suggestions, ideas, and tips to kick-start a new successful business."

— FAYTHE LEVINE, director of *Handmade Nation*

"Jennifer has crafted an inspiring, informative guide for bringing creative entrepreneurial dreams to life in living color. She encourages us to see our work as art and have fun along the way. A must for all aspiring and experienced business owners' bookshelves."

— KIMBERLY WILSON, creative entrepreneur and author of
Hip Tranquil Chick and *Tranquilista*

"Are you a brilliant, intuitive entrepreneur who feels like a frustrated ostrich with your head in the sand? Jennifer Lee can help. With *The Right-Brain Business Plan*, she not only makes the world of business accessible to creative types but also shows us how to supercharge our superpowers so we surpass the left-brain competition. Viva cultural creatives!"

— KAREN SALMANSOHN, author of *How to Be Happy, Dammit*

"As we move into a time when creative visionaries are needed more than ever, Jennifer Lee's joyous, natural, and advantageous tools are more helpful than ever. Who says you can't rock Wall Street and wear purple at the same time? Jennifer Lee opens the door for artists, healers, and brilliant souls to take their passion into the marketplace — with precision and the ultimate creativity of realizing all their dreams."

— TAMA J. KIEVES, bestselling author of *This Time I Dance!:
Creating the Work You Love*, www.AwakeningArtistry.com

The Right-Brain
BUSINESS PLAN

RIGHT ☆ BRAIN
entrepreneur

May all of your
Creative Dreams
Come true!

♡ jenn

YOU + YOUR CREATIVE WORK MATTER

rightbrainbusinessplan.com

The Right-Brain
BUSINESS PLAN

A Creative, Visual Map for Success

JENNIFER LEE

FOREWORD BY CHRIS GUILLEBEAU

New World Library
Novato, California

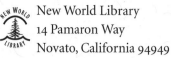
New World Library
14 Pamaron Way
Novato, California 94949

Illustrations by Kate Prentiss
Text design and typography by Tona Pearce Myers

Library of Congress Cataloging-in-Publication Data
Lee, Jennifer, date.
The right-brain business plan : a creative, visual map for success / Jennifer Lee ; foreword by Chris Guillebeau.
    p.   cm.
Includes bibliographical references and index.
ISBN 978-1-57731-944-3 (pbk. : alk. paper)
1. Business planning. 2. Creative ability in business. 3. Creative thinking. 4. Entrepreneurship. I. Title.
HD30.28.L438 2011
658.4'01—dc22   2010048864

First printing, February 2011
ISBN 978-1-57731-944-3
Printed in Canada on 100% postconsumer-waste recycled paper

New World Library is a proud member of the Green Press Initiative.

10   9   8   7   6   5   4   3

This book is dedicated to right-brain entrepreneurs everywhere who are courageously pursuing their creative passions. You rock!

Contents

Chapter 5
Managing the Moola — Color by Numbers

Chapter 6
Corralling Your Creative Cohorts

Chapter 7
Action Planning — Where the Rubber Meets the Road

Chapter 8
Weaving It All Together

Chapter 9
Maintaining the Magic and Momentum

Foreword

More than a decade ago, I said farewell to the world of conventional work and struck out to start my own business. Full speed ahead! I ordered coffee from Jamaica and sold it to connoisseurs in the United States and Canada. Over the next several years, I built a number of other small businesses that allowed me to travel and pursue my other passions. I never went back to the "real world" of employment, and what a thrill it's been.

There was just one problem: in those early days, I had no idea what I was doing. I faithfully bought a stack of business books and learned as much from them as I could. But whenever I encountered spreadsheets, financial statements, or graphs, I always turned the page as quickly as I could, or just closed the book entirely. Aside from "Make sure the income is more than the expenses," I never really had a business plan. Everything worked out in the end, but if I had known more about creative business planning in the beginning (without all the spreadsheets), I'm sure it would have been a lot easier.

It's too late for my coffee business, but it's not too late for you. In this brilliant book, Jennifer Lee shares how she always thought of herself as a *creative* but only recently as an *entrepreneur*. This illustrates an unnecessary "it has to be one or the other" limitation that many of us right-brain types apply to ourselves. Can you really be a *creative entrepreneur*? Yes, you can, and here's your field manual. When you do it on your terms instead of someone else's, running your own shop is fun and meaningful. Every day presents new challenges, and you don't have to close off the creative part of your personality to navigate them.

Jennifer's work also brings a sense of joy and adventure to a traditionally mundane process. If you think of business planning as boring, well, you haven't read this book yet. If your eyes glaze over at financial forecasts, you have nothing to fear from these pages. As far as I can tell, *The Right-Brain Business Plan* contains exactly one spreadsheet. (It's on page 115 and isn't scary at all.)

In our globalized, connected world, it has never been easier to start and run your own business. The basics are simple: You need to sell something that people want to buy. You need to practice good "Moola Management," as Jennifer would say. You need an operating plan, a strategy to get the word out, and a good idea of the kind of growth you'd like to see.

The Right-Brain Business Plan contains ideas, tools, and exercises to help with each of these areas. This is not business as usual. It's fun, creative, and purposeful. If you're looking to start or improve a small business without getting lost in the planning, you've arrived at the right place. Jump right in!

— Chris Guillebeau, author of *The Art of Non-Conformity*

Introduction

This Is Not Business as Usual

How Using Your Creative Intuition Will Make You More Successful in Business

W̶elcome, my fellow creative right-brainer, to a fun, new way of approaching business! If you're like me, the very thought of boring business plans, confusing financial statements, and anything resembling a stodgy Wall Street suit makes your skin crawl.

I used to think that creativity and business were worlds apart, especially after a decade of diligently climbing the corporate ladder while I stuffed my underappreciated creative spirit into the corner. When I finally listened to my heart and took the bold leap of quitting my day job to follow my dreams full-time, I discovered a much better way to live and work. Once I fully embraced entrepreneurship, I understood that creativity and business go hand in hand, beautifully.

The Right-Brain Business Plan maps my personal journey to joyfully integrate creativity and business in my own entrepreneurial endeavors. I'm excited to share this approach with you. Whether you're just starting out or have owned your company for years, the exercises in this book will empower you to reach magical new levels of business success as you pursue your creative passions and make your unique mark in the world.

Using Your Right-Brain Creativity to Launch and Grow Your Business

When it comes to you and business, I bet your default analytical left brain has had enough. It's been under too much pressure to "figure things out," and let's face it, you're tired of your left brain trying (desperately) to run the show. Well, guess what? In this book, you get to make best business buddies with your artistic, visionary right brain. You're invited to fully embrace your creative nature in the realm of business. Your natural right-brain gifts of imagination and intuition can actually help you find fresh solutions to your business challenges and can enable your ventures to grow in ways you never dreamed possible. You have permission to create wildly. To not be bound by what "makes sense." Isn't that how the most innovative ideas emerge?

Why Do You Need a Business Plan?

If you are in business for yourself, you are indeed an entrepreneur, even if you don't call yourself one. Just like any large company or corporation, entrepreneurs need a business plan. Sure, it may not be as complex, lengthy, or dull (thank goodness) as the business plan of a multimillion-dollar Fortune 500 organization, but it is still vital to the health of your business.

Think about it. If your business plan is a road map to your success, then not having a plan is like driving without directions to an unknown destination — yikes! You will refer to your business plan on a regular basis so that you can check where you are against your goals and adjust your course if necessary.

This book is for you if you're bored by business planning, if you find the process daunting, or if you're too busy doing what you love to bother with complex spreadsheets or lengthy templates. When planning seems unappealing, it doesn't get done, and that can derail your business. In fact, the Small Business Administration estimates that 50 percent of small businesses in America fail within their first five years. Lack of planning is often to blame. *The Right-Brain Business Plan* helps you beat the odds by providing an enjoyable, accessible, and visual approach to clarifying the big picture for your business and to developing a plan of action that will help you get the job done.

During an art challenge in November 2007, I intuitively developed my first Right-Brain Business Plan to articulate my vision and goals in a fun and creative way. My portable plan guided my business growth and inspired the approach outlined in this book.

Who Will Benefit from This Book?

If you're a budding business owner or even a seasoned entrepreneur, you'll benefit from this playful yet practical approach to turning passion into profit. Like other right-brain entrepreneurs, you might be in one of the following creative and heart-centered professions.

- You might be a creative entrepreneur, such as an artist, graphic designer, crafter, photographer, Web designer, jewelry designer, interior designer, writer, marketer, or other freelancer.
- You might be a solopreneur in one of the helping and healing professions, such as a life coach, therapist, counselor, consultant, professional organizer, teacher, leader of a nonprofit, acupuncturist, chiropractor, holistic health counselor, energy worker, yoga or Pilates instructor, or massage therapist.
- You might be an aspiring entrepreneur who is transitioning from the corporate world to working for yourself.

Or, maybe you simply know that you want to infuse fun and play into your professional work.

The Difference between Left-Brain and Right-Brain Thinking

The left brain and the right brain bring different, equally important gifts to the table. In the business world, you've probably relied on your left-brain logic to help you achieve professional success, often at the expense of your right-brain creativity. This book, however, gives you permission to let your right brain lead the way.

So what, exactly, is the difference between left-brain and right-brain thinking? Don't worry; you won't get an anatomy lesson here. But if you're interested in learning more about brain science, take a look at Dr. Jill Bolte Taylor's fascinating memoir, *My Stroke of Insight*, in which she shares her personal account of getting to know her right brain better after suffering a stroke.

The rest of us can think of it this way: You're a left-brainer if, when you're making an omelet, you read the recipe from start to finish before you even start cooking. You gather all of the ingredients ahead of time. Then you chop the onions, tomatoes, and bell peppers into precise quarter-inch cubes and place them in separate small prep bowls, then measure the half cup of cheese. Finally, you set the timer for exactly three minutes to cook the eggs.

You're a right-brainer if you open the fridge and get inspired by some vibrant red bell peppers and the scent of fresh basil. You use a bit of this and a dash of that. And then you use your intuition to cook the eggs until they're just right.

You're left-brained if you use a level and ruler to hang a picture; you're right-brained if you eyeball it.

Which description do you feel more comfortable with and identify with, and why? Does your preference differ according to the circumstances?

Your Time Is Now!

Left-brain thinking has dominated the business world for centuries; fortunately, though, dramatic shifts in our social and economic environment are leveling the playing field. As we move from a knowledge economy based on information and analysis to a creative economy built on innovation and ideas, right-brain thinking will prevail.

In his influential book *A Whole New Mind*, Daniel Pink asserts that right-brainers will rule the future (woo-hoo!). He talks about how the left-brain analytical skills that made people in the Western world successful in the past are now accessible more cheaply overseas. While left-brain thinking is still important, it's simply not enough to compete in the modern business world. Now, in order to be successful, we also need to leverage our right-brain skills. This means that abilities such as big-picture thinking, synthesizing, design, empathy, play, and creativity will help us lead the way.

Why a Right-Brain Approach to Business Planning?

Typically, we think of business planning as very much a left-brain activity, and yes, the left brain certainly does play a key role in the planning process, since it is geared for logical, analytical, critical thinking. The left brain is a rock star at solving problems, sequencing steps, and hashing out the details, all great attributes when it comes to testing a plan and carrying out the steps to make that plan happen.

The challenge is when left-brain thinking comes too early in the visioning and planning process and kills the party with its questioning, judgment, and need for every single piece of the puzzle to make absolute sense before taking that first step. This limits your thinking; good ideas are quashed before they've even had a chance to form. You get analysis paralysis. Unfortunately, this can leave you feeling frustrated, stuck, and without a plan to speak of. Sound familiar?

Fortunately, as a creative person, you're naturally gifted with right-brain intuition, imagination, and innovation. But this isn't about left-brain bashing. In fact, as you'll see throughout this book, the left brain will play an important role in different parts of your planning process. What we want to avoid is letting your left brain hijack the situation.

When you approach business planning with your right brain first, you free your mind to see creative options, explore, and find patterns and purpose. You allow yourself to dream big and to connect emotionally with your vision. When you begin with your authentic vision, you're so much better equipped to deal with all the other "stuff."

Yes, it's important to know the details and understand the numbers, but if you start from that point, you force yourself into a box and may not even get your plan finished because you become frustrated or blocked. You can always ask an expert about how to read a profit and loss statement, but you can only ask yourself about what matters most to you and your business. If you start with your vision and values, the details will follow.

How It All Got Started...

I never used to think of myself as the entrepreneurial type. Creative, yes! But when it came to running a business, I didn't know a P&L sheet from a PR campaign (well, I had some idea, but you get the picture). I did what I loved, and that was that. Yet I knew that, in order to be successful, I needed a plan.

When I fled my ten-year career in corporate America to pursue my passions full-time, one of the first things I did was check out stacks and stacks of business books from the library. All the MBA mumbo jumbo made my head spin! I took a few business classes too, but I couldn't fit my square creative business into their round traditional business models.

In my search for knowledge about how to run a business, I was overwhelmed by the intimidating details and underwhelmed by their boring delivery. I trudged along, laboriously noting my goals and plans in various documents on my computer and in my journals, but I yearned for a process that would make the planning fun.

Then along came the "Art Every Day Month" challenge. In November 2007, I participated for the first time in the annual challenge hosted by creative blogger and artist Leah Piken Kolidas: to make art every day for a whole month. After almost four weeks of immersing myself in the creative process by drawing, collaging, and painting, I was exercising my right brain regularly. Creativity infused everything I touched!

On day 29 of the challenge, I happened to be revisiting my sorry semblance of a business plan (a boring, static Word document that I hadn't looked at in more than eighteen months). With the year coming to a close, I wanted to have a clear vision of, and a plan for, where my business would be heading in the new year. Since I needed to make art that day anyway, I decided I'd get crafty about updating my business plan. I rummaged through my art supplies and found a blank accordion book. With scissors and glue stick in hand, I went to work creating a vision board for my business. I reflected on what my business stood for, imagined what new products and services I wanted to offer, whom I wanted to partner with, how I wanted to get the word out about my business, and how much money I wanted to make. I collected magazine images that helped capture my vision and glued them to the front of my accordion book. It was exciting to see the story of my business vision start to unfold.

On day 30, the final day of the "Art Every Day Month" challenge, I took my visual story one step further by adding the details that go into a traditional business plan. I added pockets and envelopes to the accordion book to hold cards that described my company and my products and services. I liked that I could pull the cards out and easily add to them, making my plan interactive and evolving. Next, I created a mini–bound calendar to list my planned events and key project milestones. I loved that the format of my plan was expandable and adaptable, just like my business. Plus, it was portable and fun to look at. Not only did my colorful plan inspire me, but it also struck a chord with other people longing to bring more of their creative spirit to their work.

Since creating my first Right-Brain Business Plan, I've expanded my business, reached most of my original professional and financial goals, and developed ways to share this intuitive approach with other creative entrepreneurs. Specifically, within the year after I completed my first Right-Brain Business Plan, I doubled my income, achieved my target number of coaching clients, led workshops regularly, appeared on television twice, and created two products: the *Right-Brain Business Plan e-Book* and the *Unfolding Your Life Vision* portable vision board kit. The following year, I started to lead workshops around the country, held teleclasses, quadrupled my distribution list, increased my online media exposure, hired a bookkeeper, and landed my first book deal. This creative approach has worked for me, and I've seen it work for hundreds of other entrepreneurs, too.

I decorated the front of an accordion book with a collage of my big vision. On the back, I captured left-brain details such as the marketing, financial, and action plans.

You Can Bet Your Bottom Dollar That Business Is Creative

As a coach and a workshop facilitator for entrepreneurial women, I've witnessed many creative business owners freeze during the planning process. A client once said to me, "Business is an uncreative process." Heavy have-tos and shoulds weighed her down and kept her stuck in inaction. As we dug a little deeper, we realized she had a long-held belief that business could only be analytical and logical. Exploring further, we uncovered that what really excited her about her business idea was the opportunity for self-expression and for making a positive impact in her community. When she connected to those core values, she was inspired to work on her business plan and manifest her vision. Now that sounds like a creative process to me!

Business is an extremely creative process. Believe me, I wouldn't be in business if I thought otherwise. It requires you to keep coming up with new ideas, products, and services and to constantly innovate to make yourself stand out. Business involves taking plenty of risks and developing creative options to choose from. And, at the heart of it, your business is a reflection of you, your values, your vision, and your voice.

? RIGHT-BRAIN REFLECTION

What limiting beliefs about business do you currently hold? How are those beliefs stifling your creativity?

One person shared the following comment on my blog: "I definitely have limiting beliefs about business, stemming from my business life most often being completely separate from my dream/creative life. I equate the word *business* with *rigidity*,... with being completely left brain–oriented,... with the idea of people forcing me to do things I hate to do." Can you relate?

Yes, business does include some tedious must-do tasks as well as the necessary planning, analysis, and decision making. Those are the *whats* that need to happen. *The Right-Brain Business Plan* also values the *how*, which can totally transform a seemingly boring or laborious exercise into a fun, creative, even joyful and inspiring experience. In this book you'll learn tools, exercises, and other creative *hows* that will help you define and plan the *whats*.

You might think business plans must look a certain way. The truth is, your business plan, especially if it's for your eyes only, can look any way you want. Think of your Right-Brain Business Plan as an artful launching pad, a playful muse, a vivid and engaging visual map that gets your creative juices flowing. The most important thing is that you understand your goals, and that you write them down on paper. We'll go into suggested formats, structure, and process in more detail in the next chapter. For now, just know that you have full permission to dream big, create passionately, and craft a plan that makes your heart sing and helps your head know where your business is going.

Right-Brain Entrepreneur Badge of Honor

As you embark on your journey of creative business planning, I invite you to proudly don this Right-Brain Entrepreneur Badge of Honor. May it remind you throughout the process that you are brilliant and talented, and that you and your creative work matter!

As a right-brain entrepreneur, I

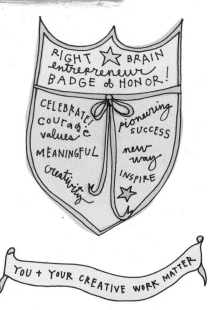

- celebrate the courage it takes to follow my heart and pursue my passions;
- define my own success;
- embrace my intuition to help me innovate, create, and problem-solve;

- inspire and empower others through my creative freedom of expression;
- live and work in alignment with my values;
- make a positive, meaningful impact with my business;
- play an important role in pioneering a new way of working that values creativity and right-brain genius.

Starting from the Top

The Skinny on the Right-Brain Business Plan
Process and Structure

Every right-brain entrepreneur needs a Right-Brain Business Plan. And a Right-Brain Business Plan needs a creative, innovative approach. This chapter will introduce you to the right-brain planning approach and will walk you through the basic building blocks of your very own visual map for success.

How to Use This Book

Think of this book as a friendly companion that will guide you through the creative planning process. You'll get lots of passionate inspiration along with practical information.

While this book focuses on right-brain techniques, it's still organized in a left-brain way. (See? The two types of thinking really do go hand in hand.) Although I've suggested a structure to follow in which each chapter builds on the one before, know that your planning process will probably be nonlinear at times. Feel free to work through the chapters sequentially, or focus in on certain topics, or skip around as you evolve and refine your plan. Make it work for you.

Developing your business plan doesn't need to take months and months of agonizing, researching, and writing — at least, not with this right-brain approach. If you prefer to dive in and get things done within a condensed time frame, and you spend a day or two on each topic (chapters 2 through 8), you can have a plan within a couple of weeks. Or, if you prefer to space things out and have more time to reflect, you can cover one topic per week and complete your plan in a couple of months.

Throughout the book, you'll find the following headings and icons:

 *Right-Brain Reflections.* Reflection questions will help you ponder, find patterns, or see the big picture. These inquiries are meant to bring your awareness to, and deepen your understanding of, a belief, intention, or situation. There are no wrong answers here, only your own personal discoveries. It's up to you how deeply you want to explore. You may want to further reflect on questions by journaling, doodling, collaging, or talking with a trusted friend, colleague, or mentor.

 Illustrated Play Sheets. Who needs serious work sheets when you can have fun, artful play sheets? Most chapters have at least one illustrated play sheet to help you explore a part of your plan in more depth. These are visual maps to guide your research, planning, and thinking using your right-brain strengths. You can also download PDF versions at Rightbrainbusinessplan.com.

Exercises. Each of the following chapters includes exercises to help you clarify your business. These exercises will help you build your right-brain muscle and may include creative art projects, daily practices, exploration, or experiential activities. They are useful for helping to inform the pieces of your plan; however, you are not required to do all of them. See what fits your business, but also stretch yourself by trying a few exercises that may seem more challenging or even aspirational. The more you explore, the more you'll learn about your business.

Right-Brain Boosters and Left-Brain Chill Pills. Sprinkled throughout are quick, healthy doses of Right-Brain Boosters to enhance your creative intuition, and Left-Brain Chill Pills to quiet your judging mind.

Tips. Occasionally, I'll offer a tip, make a suggestion, or point to something to watch out for.

Success Stories. I've included inspirational accounts of creative entrepreneurs in various stages of their businesses who've benefited from tapping into their right brains. You'll discover what worked for them as you read about their successes and experiences. I hope that, by learning from other creative entrepreneurs, you'll realize you're not alone, and that you too are a success story because you're following your dreams.

Left-Brain Checklists. Since the left brain excels at linear structure and practical details, each chapter ends with a Left-Brain Checklist to make sure all your bases are covered before you move on to the next section. Some items will be noted as optional and, depending on your business, not all of every checklist may apply to you.

Some Things to Keep in Mind

I bet that, as an entrepreneur, you're constantly doing, doing, doing to get the job done. As a right-brain entrepreneur, though, recognize that your quality of being is as important as action, if not more so. Just as the *how* is as important as the *what*, the *being* is as important as the *doing*. While you explore this process, remember the following ways of being:

- Trust your intuition.
- There is no right or wrong way to approach your Right-Brain Business Plan.

- Hold the process lightly. If you ever find yourself getting stressed out, tied up in knots, or having brain freeze, pause, take a deep breath, and ground yourself.
- If something isn't working, try something else. Anything else.
- Creative work is ever evolving. Allow things to unfold.
- It's okay to get messy.
- Have fun!

What Is a Right-Brain Business Plan?

A Right-Brain Business Plan is a visual, creative, and fun road map for your business success. Typically a business plan has yawn-inducing subheads such as "Executive Summary," "Company Overview," "Competitive Analysis," "Target Market," "Financial Plan," and "Marketing and Sales Plan." (By the way, to prevent your eyes from glazing over as you read oh-so-boring terms like these, I've taken the liberty of coming up with catchier phrases, which you'll see in a bit.) As you follow the process outlined in this book, you'll still address all these standard sections; however, you'll bring your vision and plan to life through images, art, and creative expression. You'll have a tangible representation of your business vision that can then be translated into a more formal plan, if needed.

The basic building blocks of your Right-Brain Business Plan include the following:

Hearty Highlights (a.k.a. Executive Summary). Think of this section as the CliffsNotes version of your plan. If someone needs to understand the main points of your business, she could skim this overview and get the big picture. Although I've listed this section first, your Hearty Highlights are typically written last, as they sum up the whole plan. We'll discuss Hearty Highlights/Executive Summary in chapter 8.

Business Vision and Values (a.k.a. Company Overview). This section describes what business you're in and where you're headed. Your vision

and values serve as the foundation of your Right-Brain Business Plan and connect you with what matters most to you and your business. This is also where you'll give an overview of your business, including your mission, your products and/or services, and the history of your company. Chapter 2 will walk you through this process.

Business Landscape (a.k.a. Competitive Analysis). This section describes where you fit in the marketplace, how you stand out from the competition, and where your opportunities are. In chapter 3, you'll explore the big-picture view of your industry and where you fit in. By having a clear picture of your business landscape, you'll start to clarify your customers' needs, articulate what makes you unique, and identify opportunities to grow your business. You'll also have a better idea of where to focus your time, resources, and dollars in order to make informed decisions.

Getting the Word Out (a.k.a. Marketing Plan). This section articulates who your perfect customers are and how you'll reach them. Chapter 4 will help you craft a plan and will address marketing mediums, messages, and proper timing, so you can let your perfect customers know how you can help them. This section also describes your sales process, including what process and/or support will be in place to help you seal the deal with your perfect customers.

Managing the Moola (a.k.a. Financial Plan). This section outlines how much money you need to make, how much you'll spend, and how you'll bring in the bacon. Chapter 5 guides you through a process of getting a clear picture of your financials. When you're seeking formal funding, such as a bank loan or grant, investors will go through this section with a fine-tooth comb. They'll want to know your financial projections and will examine your profit and loss statement, balance sheet, and cash flow statement. But for the purposes of your first Right-Brain Business Plan, you'll have a simple tool to help you work with the basic numbers.

Corralling Your Creative Cohorts (a.k.a. Management and Personnel Plan). Since management, personnel, and organizational structure sound way too corporate, let's think of the folks represented by these terms as your creative cohorts, the people who support you and your business. This section describes you and your qualifications, plus anyone else you need to involve in your business. Depending on the size of your creative endeavor, this may be you, the solo entrepreneur, or you may have a team of people helping you. You'll need to be clear on who does what and on how each person is getting paid. Chapter 6 will help you map out your support team.

Making Your Plan Real: Where the Rubber Meets the Road (a.k.a. Action Plan). This section highlights the steps you need to take to make your vision real and move your business forward. Chapter 7 will help you plot out the goals, strategies, and action steps necessary for implementing your business vision.

Smooth Sailing System (a.k.a. the Operational Plan). This section describes how the work gets done via your business processes, policies, and procedures. Depending on your business, this may be a simple flowchart with colorful boxes and arrows, or it may require a more complex set of steps and guidelines to deal with things like big machinery or regulations. Chapter 8 will help you with this part of the plan.

TIP

If you have multiple businesses (as many creative entrepreneurs do), use the exercises and play sheets to focus on just one business at a time, since the answers might be different for each specific venture. For example, maybe you're an art therapist who also designs inspirational jewelry. While there may be some overlap in your businesses, you'll probably find that the details differ when you identify your perfect customers for each business, the most effective ways to reach them, and how you'll earn money from each business. By focusing on one business at a time, you'll keep things simpler and more manageable. And once you go through this process for one business, it'll be easier to repeat it for the next. When you're done, you can look at both plans to see the big picture of your creative enterprise.

You'll notice that there are plans within the plan. The entire Right-Brain Business Plan is the umbrella, and, beneath it, specific sections (such as "Getting the Word Out" and "Managing the Moola") help you map out the details for the various aspects of your business. As you move through this process, you'll also notice that the different sections may overlap or cross-reference each other. For example, "Managing the Moola" is informed by what type of marketing costs you'll have, who you might need to hire, or supplies or training you might need. That is why the planning process will be constantly evolving.

Don't get caught up in deciding whether something needs to go in one section rather than another. The important thing is to get your thoughts on paper so you have something to respond to.

I just highlighted the basic building blocks that go into a Right-Brain Business Plan, but every business is different, which means there isn't a cookie-cutter approach. This book will provide key questions to consider when planning a business, but take into account your unique situation and make adjustments as needed.

Using her own whimsical drawings, acrylic paint, colorful paper, glitter, and feathers, artist and author Violette Clark transformed a children's picture book into a festive visual plan.

Use Your Creative License When Choosing a Format for Your Visual Plan

The Right-Brain Business Plan breaks the traditional business-planning mold by inviting you to bring your vision to life through pictures, colors, and other forms of self-expression. So, here's the cool deal ... your Right-Brain Business Plan can look any way you want! Hallelujah!

I've suggested various formats here to inspire you as you construct your plan. Also, to spark your muse, you'll read about some innovative entrepreneurs who infused their Right-Brain Business Plans with lots of creative license.

You don't necessarily need to know right now what the end product of your plan is. The exercises in each chapter will help the format and details evolve. The most

Let your creative juices flow, as consultant and teacher Pascale Rousseau did when she set an intention for her business vision by intuitively drawing a mandala.

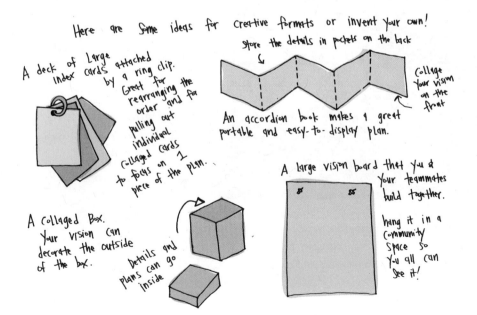

Here are some ideas for creative formats or invent your own!

A deck of large index cards attached by a ring clip. Great for rearranging the order and for pulling out individual collaged cards to focus on 1 piece of the plan.

Store the details in pockets on the back

An accordion book makes a great portable and easy-to-display plan.

Collage your vision on the front

A large vision board that you & your teammates build together.

hang it in a community space so you all can see it!

A collaged Box. Your vision can decorate the outside of the box.

Details and plans can go inside

important thing is to get your ideas from your head out into the world, in whatever creative form that takes. If, however, you do like knowing ahead of time what the finished piece will be like so you can gather the right materials and supplies, here are some ideas people have used to create their Right-Brain Business Plans:

- An accordion book with pockets and cards
- A large poster board for a collage on the front and notes on the back
- A collaged box with cards and details inside
- Index cards and envelopes
- Index cards tied together with a ribbon
- A visual journal or sketchbook
- An altered book
- A mural, drawing, portrait, or painting
- A mandala
- A handmade piece of jewelry
- A hanging wall piece or mobile made out of paper plates and string
- A diorama or shadow box
- A scrapbook
- A storyboard or comic strip
- A quilt
- A video montage
- A bulletin board

Coach Ana Ottman of Red Dress Studios helps women entrepreneurs build their confidence muscles. Her bold vision board (one panel shown here) empowers her to confidently put herself out there and take risks, too.

- A sculpture
- An installation piece

The sky's the limit! Maybe consider a combination of mediums: one to illustrate your big-picture vision (like a vision board or a bracelet), and another to capture all the information that supports the vision (perhaps index cards bound together with ribbon). Part of what makes the Right-Brain Business Plan delightful is creating all the accoutrements that communicate the details with style and flair. You can also take a peek at chapter 8 for some additional ideas for fun formats or check out the featured business plan spotlights on Rightbrainbusinessplan.com.

RIGHT-BRAIN REFLECTION

What other innovative ideas do these suggestions spark for you? What are you inspired to create?

Other Materials for Your Visual Plan

Besides the supplies you'll need to make your Right-Brain Business Plan, you will also want to have some of these other materials handy to do the creative exercises throughout this book:

- A journal
- Magazines
- Scissors
- Glue sticks
- Tape
- Paper
- Colorful markers, pens, or colored pencils

- Highlighters
- Sticky notes (in an assortment of colors, including yellow, pink, and green, and different sizes)
- Index cards
- A computer
- A color printer

SUCCESS STORY

Lauren Brownstein of Pitch Consulting, LLC, provides fundraising and consulting services to nonprofit organizations, offering them grant-writing, training, and campaign support. She dished up her annual business goals in the form of a mobile made out of paper plates. On the individual plates she made collages with titles such as "What do my clients experience?" and "Who are my business partners?" Then she wrote the details of her plan on the backs of her collages, punched holes in the plates, tied them all together with string, and proudly hung her colorful mobile by her desk, where she couldn't miss it. In the nonprofit world, where grants must follow strict guidelines and consultants work themselves into the ground, her fun-loving business plan reminded Lauren that she didn't always have to follow the rules. She could enjoy a playful attitude while still delivering laser-focused, top-notch results and an excellent customer experience. In addition to setting financial and work goals, she included her lifestyle goals, like being able to travel, setting a nontraditional schedule, and appreciating the spirituality in her work. With her mobile Right-Brain Business Plan, Lauren's goals soared to new heights!

Keep your motivation high by hanging your Right-Brain Business Plan in plain sight, as nonprofit consultant Lauren Brownstein of Pitch Consulting did with her clever paper-plate mobile.

- Other art supplies based on your preferred medium
- A bulletin board with pushpins or magnets (optional)
- Large sheets of paper or flipchart pads (optional)
- Paint (optional)
- Paintbrushes (optional)
- Digital camera (optional)
- If you like organizing your papers in binders, try Levenger's Circa notebooks instead of the clunky three-ring office-store variety; these special notebooks allow you to easily move pages around and add tabs and pockets in a more elegant format (see the Resources section for more information; optional)

RIGHT-BRAIN REFLECTION

Before jumping in, spend ten minutes journaling about what's worked in your business to date. What approaches have been successful? If you are new to your business, jot down some reflections on what's worked for you in previous jobs or what your natural gifts are. This will be helpful to come back to when you start to carry out your plan.

The Many Ways You Can Use Your Right-Brain Business Plan

Your Right-Brain Business Plan serves several different purposes. You can use it to do the following:

Know where you're headed. Most important, your business plan helps you get to where you want to go on your entrepreneurial journey. It's a road map that articulates your vision and the detailed steps needed to bring your vision to life. It helps you track how well you're doing against your goals. And, to make decisions that align with your overall vision, you can check in with your plan as you would with a trusted confidant.

By taking the time to create your plan, you show that you're committed to your success and that you mean business.

Test out your ideas. The exercises in this creative planning process can serve as a safe laboratory in which to test out how solid your plan is before you invest loads of time and cold, hard cash. Just as a painter uses a sketchbook to scribble notes, practice techniques, and dabble in ideas before committing the final image to canvas, you can use your Right-Brain Business Plan to experiment, ask yourself the important questions, and get feedback about how your business will work.

SUCCESS STORY

Leave it to the brilliant Bevla Reeves of HairConspiracy.com, an online resource for high-end clip-in hair extensions, to craft a cool Right-Brain Business Plan. Bevla had fun turning her annual business goals into a crystal-studded leather cuff bracelet. Every time she wears it, she's reminded of her sparkly seven-point plan to success. Plus, the bracelet is a great conversation piece that gives her plenty of opportunities to promote her business. Like I said, brilliant! The Right-Brain Business Plan inspired Bevla to reconnect with her creativity, have fun, and fall in love with her business all over again, as she did when she first launched it. Some of the goals she's accomplished include adding new products to her line, getting a business loan, establishing connections with suppliers in Asia, adding video to her site, and reinstating her marketing plan. How's that for a Right-Brain Business Plan that shines?

Bevla Reeves's bejeweled bracelet succinctly reminds her of her HairConspiracy.com business goals.

Home in on a specific aspect of your business. If you already have an established business or a business plan, you can use the Right-Brain Business Plan process to help you map out the specifics of a particular new service or product. Perhaps you want to create a plan for a new class you'll be offering, or you want to add to your line of merchandise, or you're expanding your home business to include a rented office or a retail space. You can use your plan to gain clarity on a distinct segment of your business.

Stay inspired. Unlike traditional business plans, your Right-Brain Business Plan is not a dull, dense, three-inch binder that merely collects dust on your bookshelf. Instead, your plan is a fun, visual representation to display proudly and play with often. By connecting with your unique work of art regularly, you'll be inspired to bring your vision to life.

Get your creative cohorts on board. Not only will your Right-Brain Business Plan inspire you, but it will inspire others, too. Your business plan is a valuable tool for communicating your vision to other people, including your team, business partners, and employees. Do a "show and tell" with your creative cohorts to engage them in your vision, and ask them to help you make it happen. Refer to your plan to help educate your team about the ins and outs of your business, products, services, policies, and procedures. Use your plan to help you track your progress with your inner circle of advisors (we'll talk more about your inner circle later).

Ask for money. Perhaps your business is at the stage where you require funds from a bank, a granting agency, investors, or potential business partners in order to grow. Your Right-Brain Business Plan will help you clarify your financial picture. While you may not want to saunter into a bank meeting with your colorful magazine cutouts and vision board in hand, you can certainly use the creative exercises outlined in this book as a jumping-off place. A more standard framework is provided in chapter 8 for when you need a more buttoned-down version. The document will be easy to fill in once you've gone through the exercises in this book.

Even if your one-person business doesn't require investors right now, it's always good to have a clear picture of your business and what you might need financially in the future.

Whether your plan is for your eyes only or designed to get others on board, it is going to be a valuable resource as you grow your business.

RIGHT-BRAIN REFLECTION

What do you intend to use your Right-Brain Business Plan for? What do you hope to gain from creating your plan?

What will your plan focus on?

- Launching a new business.
- Growing an existing business.
- Planning specifically for a new product.
- Planning specifically for a new service offering.
- Other?

Do you intend to ask for money (such as a bank loan, investment, etc.)?

- Yes.
- No, my plan is just for me to know where I'm headed.
- I'm not sure right now.

Have you created a business plan before?

- Yes.
- No.

What intimidates you about doing a business plan?
What excites you about doing a business plan?
What is your biggest challenge as an entrepreneur?
What is your biggest strength as an entrepreneur?
What's the most important thing you want to take away from this process?

Your intentions will help you focus throughout the planning process on what's most important for you and your business.

Now that you have a sense of the overall approach, let's get started. The next chapter will help you get in touch with the big vision of your business.

Crafting Your Business Vision and Values

Where Is Your Business Headed, and What Do You and Your Company Stand For?

Your work, like that of most creative entrepreneurs, authentically expresses who you are. You set up shop because you want to do things your own way and make your unique impact on the world. Your creative business reflects your vision, values, and voice.

Your *vision* is the big picture of your business (and your life). It's where you see yourself heading and includes how you're making a positive difference, what success looks and feels like to you, and what makes life and work ripe with fulfillment and meaning.

Your *values* are what you hold as most important to you. Values are your lifeblood. Values are what make you tick. Many solopreneurs honor their personal values through their work, so your business values may be based on your personal ones.

Your *voice* is the unique way in which you show up in the world. Your authentic voice helps you stand out from the crowd. If your vision is the big picture you're painting, and your values are the colorful paints, then your voice is like the beautiful brushstroke you use to bring your vision to life.

These cornerstones of your business — your vision, values, and voice — will help guide you in making the decisions that are right for you and your business, and in this chapter, you'll get to explore each of them.

Artist and workshop leader Michelle Casey stays connected to her Big-Vision Collage by using the inspiring image as a screen saver on her computer and mobile phone.

Vision: Start with Heart

The first step in creating your Right-Brain Business Plan is to connect wholeheartedly with the vision of where you're heading in your business and life. While many traditional business books espouse starting a business by evaluating the external environment, your Right-Brain Business Plan begins by looking internally — at what has heart and meaning for you. You'll use your creative, visual, emotional, and intuitive right brain to imagine what you desire and what's possible (or seemingly impossible!).

Think about why you wanted to start your own business in the first place. If you're like most creative entrepreneurs, your work is a labor of love, you crave more autonomy or life balance, and you want to have passion and purpose in what you do. You might also use your work to make a positive difference in the world around you. All these aspects and more make up your vision. In the following guided visualization, you'll explore your ideal day, desired business accomplishments, new offerings, your work space, perfect customers, financial abundance, and the legacy you want to leave.

While you may come up with a grand, detailed vision, make sure you hold it lightly. Your business may grow and unfold in unexpected ways. You'll gravitate toward things that you can see more clearly because you know what you're looking for. And by simply moving forward, you'll unearth many hidden opportunities that will unexpectedly enhance your business and your life. The more connected you are to your vision, the more likely you will keep progressing toward it and will manifest it.

EXERCISE

Dream Big with the Big-Vision Visualization

To fully access your creative intuition, make sure you find a place where you can be completely relaxed and uninterrupted while you visualize. Turn off the ringer on your phone. Post a Do Not Disturb sign so your family won't bother you. Light a candle or burn some incense to set a mellow mood.

In this relaxed space, give yourself permission to let your imagination roam freely. There is no right or wrong here. As you listen to the guided meditation, you might have an epic vision filled with colorful

TIP

To fully immerse yourself in the experience, have a friend slowly read the following visualization script to you, record yourself reading it, or download an MP3 recording of the Big-Vision Visualization from Rightbrainbusinessplan.com.

details, or you may simply experience an inkling or a feeling. Either is perfectly fine. Also, you don't need to take everything that you see literally. Your right brain may be speaking to you in symbols and metaphor, so allow yourself to interpret the deeper meaning later, if needed.

Each time you do this exercise, you might experience something slightly different, and that's okay. It doesn't mean the original vision you had isn't valid anymore; it may just mean you're accessing another part of your imagination and expanding what's possible, or that you have a new sense of clarity. It may also take a few rounds of visualization to really sink your teeth into the exercise. And finally, don't beat yourself up if things are fuzzy. There will be plenty of other exercises to help you tap into the various aspects of your vision, so trust that your big-picture dreams will sharpen over time.

Big-Vision Visualization Script

Find a nice comfortable position, either sitting up or lying down. Let your eyes close. Allow yourself to take some gentle, deep breaths in and out. With each inhale, breathe in creativity and vitality. With each exhale, let go of any tension or worry. Again, breathe in deeply. Good. And breathe out completely.

What does your ideal day look like?

What parts of that day bring you the most joy and fulfillment?

As you connect with your breath, start to notice what sensations you feel in your body. You might become aware of your belly rising and falling with each breath. Just relax your entire body, allowing yourself to be fully supported by the ground or seat beneath you. You might start to feel a tingling sensation in your fingers and toes. Allow that tingling sensation to begin radiating throughout your entire body, through every muscle, as it melts away any tension or worry. Let the tingling sensation radiate up your torso and back, up your neck and up through the crown of your head. Let it run down your shoulders and arms, and out the tips of your fingers, allowing you to relax even more. Then let the tingling radiate down your pelvis, legs, and feet to the tips of your toes. As you let these soothing sensations radiate through each and every cell of your body, you become more and more peaceful and calm.

Now that you feel completely relaxed, allow yourself to imagine that it is some time in the future. A year from now, two years, five years — it's up to you. This is your opportunity to experience the success and abundance of your business in the future.

To start this journey, allow yourself to picture where you do your work. See the space where you turn your dreams into reality, where you pursue your passions, where you make a difference.

Notice what is around you. Look around and take in what this environment is like. Is it large and expansive? Or small and intimate? What are the colors, textures, and smells of this place? What is the energy like? Is it exciting and thrilling? Is it serene and grounding? Or perhaps inspirational and uplifting?

Take in the details...What are the materials in this space? What do you surround yourself with?

Now, go to a specific spot in this work space. Perhaps it's a table and chair, a counter, a spot on a stage or in front of an easel, or a seat at a desk or by a computer. Maybe it's outside in the open air, in the expanse of nature. Visualize wherever it is that you can truly engage with your work. Take in the essence of this specific spot. What does it tell you about your business and how you run it?

Now take a look around you. Do you work alone, or are there other people with you, perhaps coworkers, customers, friends, family, partners? Who are they, what are they doing, what's their energy like? What do they say about working with you? What impact do you have on them?

Now allow yourself to connect with what brings you the most joy and fulfillment in your work in the future. What is it that you truly enjoy about your business? What values are you honoring in your work? How are they a reflection of what your company is known for? What legacy are you leaving through your work?

When you feel totally connected to your vision — as if you're living and breathing it TODAY — you've harnessed the power of the **right-brain BUSINESS plan**

Allow yourself to imagine that your business is wildly successful and overflowing with abundance. You are earning money easily and effortlessly, doing what you love. You can even picture people happily paying you again and again for your work. What do you notice about wealth and abundance in your business in the future? What do you enjoy spending your earnings on?

In addition to your financial success, you have achieved your goals and dreams. What successes and milestones have you celebrated? What awards or recognition have you received? What is new or different in your business? What new products or services are you offering? How have you grown, expanded, or evolved?

Really allow yourself to take in the full experience of living and breathing your work in the future. Know that it is a reflection of who you are, a representation of your values, voice, and vision.

Feel free to take another look around this special place where you do your work. What else do you notice? Just let your senses drink in the sights, sounds, and smells of this place. What special details do you want to make sure you remember?

Before you get ready to come back to the present time, do what you need to in order to say good-bye to this wonderful place of work, and know that you can come back and visit anytime you wish.

In a few moments, we'll count back from three to one. At the count of one, you will be awake and renewed, knowing you can remember everything you need to of your future vision.

Three. Coming back now. Becoming more awake and alive. Two. Wiggling your fingers and toes, moving your body and feeling the temperature of your skin. And one. Eyes open, feeling totally awake and renewed.

LEFT-BRAIN CHILL PILL

It's normal to feel excited but also scared, overwhelmed, or confused by your big vision. If you find yourself worrying about how you're going to accomplish your big vision or when you'll ever have a crystal-clear picture, just notice that your left brain may be on overdrive, wanting everything to be ironed out pronto. Take a deep breath and trust that, as you take small steps forward, your vision will unfold.

? ∘° RIGHT-BRAIN REFLECTION

What came up in the visualization? What had heart and meaning for you? Take a moment to journal about what you experienced. Record as much detail as you can remember, including images, colors, sensations, and emotions. Talk through your visualization with a trusted friend. Have her ask you open-ended, curious questions, such as "What was that like?" "What did you notice?" or "How did that feel?" to help deepen your exploration.

Allow yourself to imagine what else is possible. It doesn't have to make sense or even seem feasible at this point. Remember, creativity, intuition, and big-picture thinking fuel your right brain.

EXERCISE

Recapping Your Visualization

Write notes about your visualization on an index card or piece of paper (you can add this to your Right-Brain Business Plan later). Include as much detail as you can remember. Bring your future vision to the present by using the present tense. Here are some prompts to help you:

I am proud of _____.

It feels _____ to have accomplished _____.

I am honoring my values, which are:

_____.

I set myself apart by _____.

If you have someone to do this exercise with, you can each take a turn sharing what came up for you. When you're through sharing, write down any other notes on your card.

RIGHT-BRAIN BOOSTER

To turn the sharing experience up a notch, throw in some improvisation and act out your vision, using your whole body and emotions.

RB BOOSTER

Alternative Exercise

If guided visualizations aren't your cup of tea, here's an alternative exercise. Get a pen and paper and set a timer for ten minutes. Allow yourself to write freestyle about where you see your business and life in the future. Keep your pen constantly moving. Don't pause to think about what's next or stop to edit. Don't worry if it doesn't make sense or has grammatical errors or misspellings. You aren't going for a Pulitzer here. Rather, you want to tap into your creative flow. If you get stuck, quickly shake your whole body and accompany the movement with sound, and then keep writing. When the timer rings, put your pen down and, with compassionate curiosity, look over what you just jotted down (kicking any critical cattiness to the corner). What surprises you about what you wrote? What excites you? Where can you take it further?

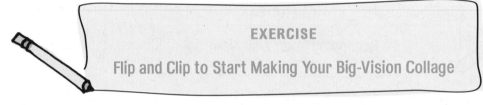

EXERCISE

Flip and Clip to Start Making Your Big-Vision Collage

Now we'll start bringing your vision to life with a collage.

What you'll need:

- Magazines, photographs, junk mail, catalogs, or marketing materials that inspire you
- Glue stick
- Scissors
- A surface to collage on, such as one side of an accordion book, a piece of card stock, or a poster board

Instructions: Thumb through your magazines and other material for images that evoke what you discovered in your vision (or journaling). Cut or tear out pictures and words that represent the images and feelings you experienced. Let yourself be drawn to things that weren't in your visualization, but that somehow speak to you. That's your intuition in action once more. Don't edit yourself. Go on a scavenger hunt for images and inspiration. Let the images and words resonate with you emotionally. Collect your clippings in piles or spread them out around you.

Group Your Images

Once you've collected all your images, it's time to start grouping them. You don't have to glue things down just yet. Just start arranging your images to tell the story of your business. Organize your clippings in any way that feels right to you.

You can group your images into general categories like the ones suggested or create your own. You might see that your images will start to naturally organize themselves into a progression that has meaning to you.

Suggested categories:

- Company overview
- Values (if you want to make cards that illustrate your values, instead of including values in your Big-Vision Collage, see the card deck exercise later in this chapter)
- Perfect customers (there will be a more detailed exercise in chapter 4, if you want to save your clippings for that)
- Products and services
- Wealth and abundance
- Getting the word out
- Creative cohorts

Once you have a feel for the flow, then you can start gluing the images down. As discussed in chapter 1, you can use whatever format you'd like for your Right-Brain Business Plan. Your Big-Vision Collage can be on a large poster, on one side of an accordion book, on index cards, or on any other medium you fancy.

If you don't use all your clippings, store the extras in an envelope,

TIP

Sometimes people can get so caught up in the excitement of collecting images and searching for the absolute perfect assortment of pictures that they never move beyond the gathering phase. Set a time limit for yourself, and trust you'll find all you need within that window. Put on some inspiring or energizing music that will play for up to two hours, and when the music stops, put down your magazines and scissors. Remember, you can always come back to the exercise later. Collage allows you to layer images as you go.

folder, or box so they will be accessible later, in case you want to either use them or just look at them for inspiration or ideas. You can always add images to other parts of your plan, so don't feel like you need to squeeze everything into this Big-Vision Collage. Just as you can't do everything in your business, don't try to do everything here: focus on what matters most to you.

SUCCESS STORY

Mary Daniel Hobson is an artist who works in mixed-media photography. In her Big-Vision Visualization, Mary Daniel saw a beam of light that illuminated the middle of her studio and infused her hands with a creative, healing energy that flowed into her artwork. The beam of light became the center of her vision and connected her to her creative power. For her collage, she found an image of a crystal to represent that energy and placed it in the center of her vision book. All the other pieces of her business and personal life stemmed from that core.

When Mary Daniel started to feel frustrated or constricted by some of the more left-brain financial and marketing aspects of her business, she reconnected with her Big-Vision Collage and immediately knew on an intuitive level what felt right. She knew that in order to be successful on her terms, she didn't have to push herself to do things she didn't want to do. Instead she focused on her passion and what lit her up.

To symbolize a powerful beam of light she saw in her visualization, artist Mary Daniel Hobson placed an image of a crystal in the center of her Big-Vision Collage. When she looks at this image, she reconnects with the creative, healing energy she experienced in her vision.

She looked to her collage to show her the next steps and to help her trust her inner voice. Doing so helped her keep moving forward with her art and getting herself out there in a gentler, more authentic way.

SUCCESS STORY

Art teacher Julie Benjamin dreamed of opening up her own art studio for kids. Imagining the details of the space energized her, so her Big-Vision Collage captured the style, essence, and feel of the studio. She envisioned a large wooden table to represent grounding, community, and a wide-open space for creativity. She found a picture of a table and placed it prominently on her collage. Soon after, she discovered the perfect location to open up Little Lane Studios. As the space was getting fixed up, she brought in a special wooden table that became a centerpiece and metaphor for her business.

Copyright © Tinywater Photography www.tinywater.com

Julie Benjamin's vision board and her values — community, creativity, and collaboration — were catalysts that enabled her to launch her big dream, Little Lane Studios (shown here), an art studio for children.

As the success stories of Mary Daniel (page 40) and Julie (above) show us, this Big-Vision Collage will be the foundation for your business. It represents where you want to take your business and is the inspiration you'll come back to as you build the other supporting pieces of your Right-Brain Business Plan. If you're doing an accordion book, it's helpful to have this big-picture vision on the front; on the back you can include details illustrating the information you gather while reading the following chapters. Or, as with Julie's Right-Brain Business Plan, your Big-Vision Collage might be on a large piece of paper that you hang in your work space, and you might collect other information in a separate notebook or journal. Whenever you find yourself getting tense or worried about how to answer the more detailed questions that follow in the next chapters, come back to your Big-Vision Collage and reconnect with the feelings generated by your big vision.

Your values play an important role in your business. They are what you and your business stand for. And they are what your customers will experience when they interact with your company — which may entail anything from reading a simple marketing message, to engaging in a personal session with you, to using your product. Values will also help you make decisions. Are you honoring your values and your business goals with the decisions you're making?

If you're a solopreneur, your business values will most likely reflect your individual values. To identify your core values, reflect back on times in your life when you were on top of the world. These are discrete moments when you felt fully alive. For one client, it was when she experienced the thrill of skydiving. Adventure, it turned out, was really important to her, and she wanted more of it in her life. Your special moments could be ones you experienced while winning a high school track tournament, while backpacking in Europe with friends during summer break, or while simply taking a walk along the beach or playing with your dog. In these moments of feeling really fulfilled and happy, who were you being? What was going on around you? What were you doing? How can you bring those elements into your work and business right now?

Articulating your values, as artist Violette Clark did, will ensure that you align your business with what's most important to you.

Write down your answers or talk through your examples with a friend, and ask your friend to take notes for you so you can stay in the moment.

Befriend (Don't Banish) Anger: Uncover Its Clues to Your Values

Another way to identify your values is to look at what frustrates or upsets you. Anger often indicates a trampled value, a misdirected passion, or a violated boundary. When you're feeling unsatisfied, chances are you're not honoring some core value.

Think of specific times when you were mad or frustrated. What was happening? What about these situations upset you most? Write down your descriptions of them. To find your values, flip the words or phrases around to focus on what's most important to you. For example, if you get annoyed when someone asks you about something he could figure out for himself, perhaps you value resourcefulness, independence, or taking care of oneself. Make a list of the new words or descriptions to identify additional possible values. Your values might be a string of words, such as "beauty/creativity/uniqueness" or "freedom/independence/solitude."

The more insight you have into yourself, the more insight you'll have into your business. Running a business is as much a personal-growth journey as it is a professional endeavor. Values are one of the ways that you get to express yourself through your work, and how fulfilled you feel is an indicator that your work is aligned with your values. As a right-brain entrepreneur, you'll find that, if your values are not reflected in your work, your work will lack meaning. Are you being authentic in your business? If you're compromising your values, you'll feel resentful, upset, burned out, and frustrated. When you're aligned with your values, you'll feel fulfilled and energized, and that is what people will resonate with most.

EXERCISE

Create a Card Deck of Your Values

Using the lists of words and descriptions from your values exploration, narrow down your top five to ten values or values strings. Next you'll be creating a visual reminder of your values by collaging a card for each value or values string.

What you'll need:

- Index cards (either 4" x 6" or 5" x 7")
- Magazines

Creating values cards allows you to consciously honor one value at a time.

- Scissors
- Glue stick
- Pens
- Hole punch (optional)
- Loose-leaf ring or ribbon to hold cards together (optional)
- A small easel to display your cards (optional)
- Laminator, such as a Xyron machine, to protect your cards (optional)

Instructions:

- Write a value or values string on each index card.
- Look through magazines to find images that represent your values.
- Cut them out and paste them on the appropriate index card. You could also cut out the actual value words and collage them on the front of your card.
- If you want to keep them bound together, you can punch a hole in the corner of each card and attach them with a ring or with ribbon.
- If you'd like to protect your collages, consider laminating them. You can do it yourself with a

RIGHT-BRAIN BOOSTER

Get up and move your body. Shake your arms and legs. Circle your hips. And hey, while you're at it, make some noise, like a sigh or maybe even a roar. That's sure to help you find your voice.

RB BOOSTER

Xyron sticker maker, using the laminator cartridge, or take your cards to a copy center and have it done for you.

If you'd like, you can simply include your values on a section of your Big-Vision Collage. The nice thing about having them on separate cards, though, is that you can focus on each one individually.

Voice: Your Passion and Purpose Proclamation (a.k.a. Mission Statement)

So you have a sense of your vision, and you've articulated your values. Now it's time to fine-tune your voice so you can speak more confidently about what you do. Most business books have you create a mission statement, where you state why your company exists and why people would want to buy from you. With your Right-Brain Business Plan, you'll use your vision and values to help you pen a Passion and Purpose Proclamation instead. This proclamation describes what has heart and meaning for you and your perfect customers, and how you're making a positive impact through your work. Through your proclamation, you claim your unique gift and impact on the world, and you manifest them by means of your career or calling. How cool is that?

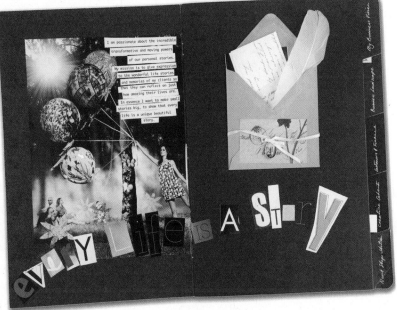

Custom book designer and storyteller Tanya Demello of My Little Life tells the story of her business through her inspiring Passion and Purpose Proclamation and tagline.

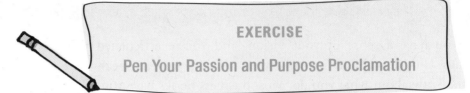

Take time to journal about the following questions. What has heart and meaning for you? What lights you up? What do you want to accomplish with your business? What's the difference (big or small) that you want to make in the world? What mark will you leave on the world by running your business?

EXERCISE

Pen Your Passion and Purpose Proclamation

Your Passion and Purpose Proclamation need only be a few lines. The simpler it is, the better, but don't get caught up in wordsmithing it to death. The point here is just to capture the essence of what brings you alive and what impact you want to make with your work.

To help you start drafting your proclamation, complete the following sentences:

- I am passionate about...
- My purpose is to...

Example of a massage therapist's proclamation: I am passionate about health, well-being, self-care, and relaxation. My purpose is to help people find ease and comfort in their own skin through the healing power of massage.

Another way to approach the purpose part of the proclamation is to play with metaphors and similes to get you out of your logical mind and into your imagination. What's a metaphor for your business and the impact you're making? If your business were an animal, a location, a color, or a song, what would it be, and why? For example: My business is a butterfly because it helps people transform. Or: My business is a cheetah because speedy service is our top priority. Or in the case of the massage therapist: My business is a warm ocean breeze that soothes the soul.

Your Passion and Purpose Proclamation expresses how you want yourself and your business to show up in the world. Make sure you write your proclamation out and include it on your Big-Vision Collage, on a card that you can place in your Right-Brain Business Plan, or in some other visible spot so you can connect with it often.

Setting Your Solid Foundation

You've done an excellent job of setting a solid foundation for your creative business by crafting your big vision, articulating your values, and fine-tuning your voice. In the next chapter, you'll explore your business landscape and how you fit in. As you start to turn your gaze outward, the internal work you did here will keep you grounded in what matters most to you.

- Listen to the Big-Vision Visualization, and journal what came up for you.
- Create your Big-Vision Collage.
- Identify your core values. Make a values card deck (optional).
- Pen your Passion and Purpose Proclamation.

LEFT-BRAIN CHECKLIST

Before moving on to the next chapter, review the checklist below. Your left brain will thank you!

- ❏ I have connected with the big vision of my business.
- ❏ I have created, or started to create, my Big-Vision Collage.
- ❏ I have articulated my core values.
- ❏ I have drafted my Passion and Purpose Proclamation.

Painting Your Business Landscape

It's a Big World Out There —
Where Do You and Your Business Fit In?

As a creative entrepreneur, you could happily spend all day in your studio painting, at your computer writing, or otherwise completely immersing yourself in your meaningful work. It's your love of what you do that drives you. When it comes to crafting a business plan, though, you must also ensure that your passions intersect with what people are willing to pay for. You can have a great idea, but if there's no market for it you won't have a successful business. And, even if there is a market, other businesses are out there competing for the same dollars in your potential customers' wallets.

This means that, in addition to pursuing your passion, you need to understand the relevant business landscape. This is the big-picture view of your industry and where you fit in.

Several different elements make up your business landscape. You'll be looking at both external and internal elements.

The external elements are outside your control (no matter how much you'd like to control them!):

- The group of potential and existing *customers* who need and would be willing to buy your products or services are what corporate business-types generally call "the market."
- *Trends* are the social, economic, environmental, or technological buzz about what's hot in the market right now.
- Your *competition* includes your peers and other businesses that serve your market and vie for your customers' attention and dollars.
- *Barriers* or obstacles get in the way of your entering a market. These could include the need for lots of moola to launch the business, distribution challenges, or the fact that consumers are not ready for what you have to offer. If you find a way to address these obstacles, then you have a leg up on your peers.

The internal elements are things that are under your control. These include the following elements:

- *Strengths:* what you're naturally good at, what makes you stand out.
- *Challenges:* where you might be falling short of the competition.
- *Opportunities:* where you might have a leg up, based on your strengths and your competitors' challenges.

LEFT-BRAIN CHILL PILL

LB

I know all this talk about the viability of your business can feel intimidating, and your judging mind is probably having a field day. This is why a lot of people don't get past the initial research. But if in the process of examining the business landscape you discover obstacles or get discouraged, this doesn't mean you must give up on your big dreams. What you want to avoid is letting your entrepreneurial endeavor sap all your energy and resources. Instead, you'll want to focus on joyfully finding creative opportunities to help you make your business work for you. By doing your homework in a right-brain way, you'll gain more insight into making your business work, so stick with it. It's actually not as bad as you might think.

We'll be exploring each of these elements in more detail throughout the chapter, and I'll introduce you to a few right-brain approaches to gathering and analyzing the data.

But How Am I Supposed to Know All This?!

Yikes, in that last paragraph, did you just read "gathering and analyzing the data"? Yes, you did. But not to worry: during this research process, you have full permission to take many SWAGs (a consultant's term meaning "silly wild-ass guesses"). You may feel like you're pulling things out of thin air, and that is A-OK. The point is to put a stake in the ground. Trust your instincts. You know a lot more than you think you do. Plus, throughout this chapter you'll get creative guidance concerning what information to look for, how to find it, and how to make sense of it.

When you start scribbling notes, filling out the play sheets, and connecting the dots, you'll realize that you already have oodles of insights and ideas. And once those ideas are written on paper, then you can respond to them, refine them, and test them.

While research on the business landscape might feel analytical and left-brain, trust your right brain to follow your intuition, see relationships and patterns, and take in the big picture. Sometimes there will be a series of related questions, but don't get overwhelmed. These merely provide different perspectives to help you arrive at the same answer. During your research, you may find yourself asking, "How am I supposed to know that?" Don't panic! It doesn't mean you can't move forward. Rather than stay stuck, take a SWAG. You can always come back later and refine your responses as you learn more.

As with any part of your Right-Brain Business Plan, painting the picture of your business landscape is an ever-evolving process. You may start by researching your peers and then move on to identifying hot topics. One section informs another. It's not linear, so don't worry about finishing one piece thoroughly before moving on to the next. Just keep daubing your paint here and there until the picture starts to form.

Mr. Monk Meets Claude Monet

In this chapter you'll play both detective and artist. It's sort of like private investigator Adrian Monk meets Impressionist painter Claude Monet. As a detective, you'll be gathering clues about the elements that make up your business landscape. You'll learn a few right-brain tools to help you do research, and then you'll break down the information you find into smaller pieces to help you analyze it. As an artist, you'll create a Business Self-Portrait, and you'll synthesize all the key details from your detective work to form your own big-picture impressions.

Play the Role of Detective: Analyze the Details and Data

Adrian Monk from the TV show *Monk* picked up as many details as he could from a crime scene and then focused on the most relevant clues to crack the case. Although Monk was a brilliant detective, he was also often sidetracked by his obsessive need for things to be clean, orderly, and perfect. (A great lesson in what *not* to do! Take the brilliant detective work but leave the OCD.) You'll be gathering clues in your own creative, lighthearted way to help paint the picture of your business landscape and determine where your opportunities lie.

Before donning your detective's hat, follow these tips for an OCD-free dive into the details:

Don't feel as if you have to do everything. The research activities described in this chapter are simply suggestions about places to look. Choose what feels most valuable and relevant to you and your business. If you're going to do a formal business plan for a loan or investment, you'll need to have a fair amount of data to back your plan. But if you're making your Right-Brain Business Plan just for yourself, don't tie yourself up in knots trying to gather every last clue.

Do your research in small chunks. Spend an hour at most on one research activity at a time — or risk having one heck of a headache!

Don't make this into "the never-ending research project." It may feel safe to stay in research mode because, if you're still gathering information, then you're not ready to take action. Or you might think of yourself as on an endless search for the elusive silver bullet that will solve all your business challenges. While the research phase is an important part of your business-planning process, make sure you give yourself a stopping point (even if your work in this section feels half-baked) and move on. You'll gain more insights as your business gets out into the world.

DETECTIVE Bulletin Board

Just as detectives use a large bulletin board with photos, newspaper clippings, and other clues to help solve a case, you'll be collecting materials from your competition, your perfect customers, and the media to make a bulletin board that will help you understand how best to position yourself. The clues will mostly focus on the external elements of your business landscape: the market, trends, and competition. You'll use the pieces you gather to compare similar businesses and find out what's working and what's not working, and to get inspired so you can decide how you might want to approach your business.

What you'll need:

- A large bulletin board with magnets or pushpins is ideal, but you can also use a large table, floor space, or, if you prefer portability, a binder, paper, and tape or staples; choose the system that works best for you
- Yellow, pink, and green sticky notes or index cards
- Highlighters, pens, and markers
- Scissors
- Computer and printer
- A printed copy of the Market and Trends play sheet downloaded from Rightbrainbusinessplan.com
- Clues such as articles, marketing material, and information about your market, trends, and competition that you'll pin up on your bulletin board; read the sections under "Collecting Clues" to find out more about what to look for and how to find it

Stay tuned: We'll come back to the Detective Bulletin Board to organize and analyze the clues later in the chapter.

Collecting Clues: What to Look For and How to Find It

The sections below suggest how to gather information about the external elements of your Business Landscape. You'll put these clues about your customers, relevant trends, and your competition on your Detective Bulletin Board to help you paint the picture of your industry.

Customers: Map Your Target Market

While we'll get to know your perfect customers in much more detail in the next chapter, it's helpful to have a sense of how big your market is. Think about the types of customers you saw in your visualization, who your favorite clients are, or folks you'd love to work with. Based on what you know about your target market so far, think about where your perfect customers might live. Search on the U.S. Census Bureau's website for statistics by state or county on things like income levels, age ranges, ethnicity, marital status, job status, and education level. If you can't track down the exact number, do you have a sense of whether there are hundreds of thousands, or thousands, or only hundreds of customers? It's helpful to know if there are enough potential customers for you to stay in business. On the flip side, you can't define your market too widely, because you won't know how to reach all the potential customers effectively. Don't worry about this too much, as you can circle back here after the next chapter.

If you need to analyze geographic information about your customers, hang up a map of your target area (for example, local, regional, state, national, and/or international) on your Detective Bulletin Board. Use pushpins of one color to indicate where you already have a customer base, and use pushpins of a different color to mark the locations where you want to be. You could also use pushpins of different colors to indicate various groupings of customers — for example, your individual clients versus your corporate clients. Or you could show where your competitors are located. Notice what geographical trends you discover. Are your customers all clustered together? Or are they far apart? How does this spread affect what you need to do to reach your target market? For example, if your customers are concentrated in one area, is a local TV

THE MARKET + TRENDS
HELP FRAME OPPORTUNITIES FOR MY BUSINESS

Look into the crystal ball...

HOW BIG IS MY MARKET?
APPROX. SIZE: _____

LOCATION:

Other information:

WHAT ARE THE SOCIAL + ECONOMIC TRENDS THAT MIGHT AFFECT MY BUSINESS?

NEWS

OTHER:

PLAY SHEET

or newspaper ad the best way to get your name out? Or, if they are dispersed across the country, are you better off with a search engine–optimized website? Make some initial guesses. You'll come back to these marketing questions in chapter 4. Are you focused on the right areas, or are there opportunities to extend into new territories? This level of demographic detail would be needed for a traditional business plan.

Clues to Add to Your Detective Bulletin Board

- Make a note of the target market number in the Markets and Trends play sheet.
- If geographic information about your customers is key to your research, consider including a map of your target area.

Social, economic, cultural, and technological trends provide insight into the changing environment. Pay attention to the trends that align with your vision and that will bolster your business. Also, use trends to help you decide when you need to let go of something that is not serving you or your customers. What trends can you capitalize on?

Some examples of current trends:

- Unemployment is at an all-time high.
- Spirituality is becoming more mainstream.
- Social online networking is becoming a more prevalent business tool.
- The "green" movement is becoming more commercial.

Keep in mind that just because something is popular doesn't mean you need to change who you are in order to fit in. Heavens, no! That would be the kiss of death to a creative person like you. Just consider what may have implications for how or where you do your business or who your customers are.

Here are some places to track trends:

- The library. Your trusty librarian can point you to relevant resources or databases.
- Books, magazines, newspapers, radio shows, TV, podcasts, and other media of interest to you and your perfect customers.
- Quickfacts.census.gov. This section of the U.S. Census Bureau's website offers easy access to statistics about people, businesses, and locations.
- Statcan.gc.ca. This is Canada's census website, which has information about people, business, locations, and more.
- Google.com/alerts. With Google Alerts, you can receive filtered information right in your inbox. Select relevant keywords or specify links you want to be notified about. Search all topics of interest to you. You can get information about your competitors, and even search your own business name or website to find out who's talking about you.

- Springwise.com. Springwise is a leading online source of new business ideas for entrepreneurs.
- Trendwatching.com. This site offers monthly trend briefings and annual reports from a leading trend firm.
- TED.com/themes. TED, which stands for Technology, Entertainment, Design, shares videos featuring some of the world's greatest thinkers as they speak on a variety of timely topics.

Clues to Add to Your Detective Bulletin Board

- Skim industry magazines and newspapers and clip articles that indicate relevant trends.
- Visit a few of the sites mentioned in this section and print out some pertinent pages to pin on your Detective Bulletin Board.
- Jot down any of your initial thoughts on trends in the trend section of the Markets and Trends play sheet.

COMPETITION: PEERING AT YOUR PEERS

For many, the word *competition* conjures up negative thoughts about win/lose, survival of the fittest, or other cutthroat calculations. In the black-and-white, left-brain world, things may need to be either/or, but in the holistic, right-brain world, there's room for more than one flavor of ice cream. While corporate suits and MBAs favor competitive lingo, the *Right-Brain Business Plan* invites you to look at businesses similar to yours as peers or colleagues who can teach you things. Throughout this book, you'll see the word *competitor* used, but please keep an open mind about what this term stands for. Your biggest competitor may even end up being the perfect collaborative partner.

By understanding what other creative entrepreneurs in your business landscape are doing, you can determine how you'll stand out from the crowd. Think of your best competitors as your virtual mentors. These are businesses whose success you'd like to emulate in your own way. Follow their progress, read their newsletters, maybe even become a customer yourself to get some official mentoring. How have they evolved their businesses? How are they marketing to their customers? This is not about copying them, as that's just not kosher. Instead, you're getting inspiration and ideas so you can figure out how to adapt messages and approaches to your unique way of doing business.

COMPETITION: ONLINE INSIGHTS

A great way to gather clues about your competitors is to surf their websites, blogs, social media sites, and reviews. Look at their online stores, price lists, product descriptions, and service offerings. If they have blogs, peruse them for comments that can give you a sense of how readers are responding to their work. How are their audiences reacting to their messages? Are the readers resonating with what your peers have to say? Do you see opportunities to bridge a gap?

Search other creative entrepreneurs' listings on Etsy, online directories, or Facebook fan pages to see what their customers are saying about them. How high are their ratings? What are customers commenting about most? Since the most satisfied and most disgruntled customers are the ones most motivated to write a review, take it all with a grain of salt. It's still information, though, and it could help you understand what's working or not working for people in the same business as you.

Check to see if there are testimonials on your competitors' websites. You can assume that the quotes represent what they

DIRECT COMPETITION AND INDIRECT COMPETITION

You may be thinking that you don't have any competition, that what you offer is unique. I have no doubt you are making a special impression in the world through your work. Potential customers, however, can choose to spend their money in various ways to fulfill their needs. You must be aware of your direct and indirect competition so that you're able to strongly communicate to your perfect customers why your option is the one they should choose.

Your direct competition offers products or services similar to yours. Think Coke versus Pepsi, Nike versus Adidas, Nikon versus Canon, or Häagen-Dazs versus Ben & Jerry's.

Indirect competition offers products and services that are different from yours but that fulfill a similar customer need. For example: a life coach versus a career counselor, a massage therapist versus a chiropractor, a hand-knitted scarf versus an embroidered silk shawl, a private yoga class versus a yoga DVD.

believe is the best about their business. This can give you insight into what this business values and what its happy, satisfied customers value. Sometimes testimonials include customers' business names, occupations, titles, or even headshots, which can give you further insight into this competitor's target market. Do they all seem to be middle-aged men who are into sports — definitely not your perfect customers? Or are they exactly your perfect customers, middle-aged moms commenting on successfully balancing work and home life?

COMPETITION: CASE THE JOINT

Conduct some detective fieldwork to gather more clues for your bulletin board. By physically getting out there, you'll have the opportunity to observe your business landscape firsthand, interact with potential customers, and gather more marketing material. Possible places to conduct your detective fieldwork include the following:

- Your competitors' offices or storefronts
- Trade shows and conferences
- Professional organization groups for your field
- Networking meetings with people in various fields
- Craft fairs
- Local shops and gift stores
- Yoga studios, massage studios, or health and wellness centers
- Expos
- Workshops, classes, or training programs

LEFT-BRAIN CHILL PILL

I have a hunch that sizing up your competition might trigger your inner critic. You know, the negative voice in your head that says things like: "Your competitor is so amazing; you'll never be as successful as she is," "You're not good enough," or "Who do you think you are?" Don't let that negative thinking get you down. Your inner critic is simply doing its job to maintain the status quo. You, the entrepreneur, on the other hand, are constantly pushing the envelope as you expand your business, so expect to hear a lot of resistance from your inner critic. To combat this nasty saboteur, remind yourself that doubt and fear are a natural part of the growth process, acknowledge that it's your inner critic talking and not you, thank your inner critic for its concern, and choose instead to focus on what you're doing well.

RIGHT-BRAIN BOOSTER

If you still find yourself in the grips of the inner critic, try these creative inner-critic busters. Write out a dialogue with your inner critic. Let it have the floor so it can get every worry off its chest. Then get curious about what's behind the fear and find a new way to relate to your inner critic. You could even get out some crayons and draw the unpleasant emotions, using colors and shapes, until you feel the negative energy dissipate. More inner-critic-busting strategies are described in chapter 9.

Also, get out and talk to existing and potential customers or conduct surveys and/or focus groups to find out more specific information. You may not be able to determine what your opportunities or your customers' needs are when you're just sitting in your office or studio trying to imagine them. But as you get out there and talk to more people, and even show what you have to offer, you'll get responses and start to understand what customers want.

While you're out and about, carry along a small notebook, camera, and/or voice recorder to capture your thoughts about what your competitors are offering and how they are offering it. What is the experience and energy of the space? What themes do you notice? What customer needs are being met? What's working or not working in these places? Document anything you want to follow up on or you think will help you improve your business.

Clues to Add to Your Detective Bulletin Board

- Go to competitors' websites and print out their home pages and any other sections of their sites that resonate with you or give you good insight into your perfect customers.
- Clip articles or ads about your competitors.
- Visit storefronts and studios and go to events, and while you're there, gather business cards, brochures, flyers, postcards, catalogs, event calendars, class schedules, newsletters, and any other marketing materials from people in your line of work or who also target your perfect customers.
- Jot down notes from your fieldwork observations.

Organizing and Analyzing Your Clues:
Detective Bulletin Board, Part 2

Now that you've gathered some clues about your business landscape, let's return to your Detective Bulletin Board and start to make sense of it all.

Organize your clues:

- Pin each item on your bulletin board, or lay all items out in front of you on a large table or on the floor. If you are using a binder, then affix each item to a piece of paper using tape or a stapler, and sort them on a table or on the floor.
- Circle or highlight keywords and whatever else on the page stands out. You might want to use some of the keywords later in your marketing messages, which we'll cover in the next chapter.
- Start grouping the items together in ways that make sense to you — for example: customer types, issues you or your customers face, hot topics, or products, services and/or companies that are similar to yours, or any other categories that are helpful.

Analyze your clues:

- Under each item (or grouping of items, depending on what level of detail you choose), you'll be placing a yellow, pink, and/or green index card or sticky note. The yellow card is for

summarizing, the pink is for what's not working, and the green is for what's working well.

- Review the item or grouping. If it's information about your competition, write on the yellow card who you think the company's target market is, what their products and services are, where they are located, how you think they reach their customers, who they might collaborate with, and any other general impressions. If it's an article about the market or trends, document on the yellow card what you think is the most important point, trend, or takeaway relevant to your business and/or your customers. For example, you may find a story saying more people are buying handmade things; this is one piece of data to support your craft business.

- If the item is information about your competition, on the pink card write what does not work about this company. What doesn't resonate with you? What would you change? This could be about their messaging, the look and feel of the brand or marketing material, their products and services, or anything else you have a reaction to. Where might they be falling short of meeting their customers' needs? What are some challenges or barriers they might face? Are these challenges similar to or different from yours? If the item is an article about the market or trends, what issues are not addressed? If you were to write a follow-up article, how would you respond? Your answers to these questions might be clues to how you are meeting a need.

- If the item is information about your competition, on the green card write what works well for this company. What do you like about their messaging, the look and feel of their brand or marketing materials, or their products and services? What are the company's strengths? How do they stand out from the crowd? What inspiring ideas did you get for your business?

- Keep repeating this note-taking process until you've covered each of the items or groupings on your board.

Take a step back and look at the various colored cards. Ask yourself the following questions:

- What themes do you notice?
- Who is your target market?
- What issues are your potential customers concerned about?
- What did you discover about your competition? What are their challenges? How have they overcome them? Identify a couple of things your peers are doing well that you might be able to adopt in your own way, or that you could do better yourself.
- What new insights have you gained by going deeper into the details?

Document your thoughts on a piece of paper and pin it to your bulletin board. These are just a few questions to get you thinking about the bigger picture. In the next section, you'll do more reflection. You'll probably keep your Detective Bulletin Board up for a while as you continue to work on the other sections of your Right-Brain Business Plan. However, when you're ready to take it down, make sure you photograph it first so you have a visual record of your process.

Play the Role of Artist: Synthesize the Patterns and Themes

Yahoo! You've made great headway in gathering clues and analyzing what those clues mean. Now that you've done such a fine job of playing detective, you can trade in your magnifying glass and investigator's hat for a paintbrush and canvas. In the role of artist, you'll look in the mirror and create a Business Self-Portrait. You'll also synthesize the clues you've gathered for the purpose of painting the picture of your business landscape and telling the story of how your business will be successful.

Just as the artist Claude Monet painted his impressions of his environment, you'll note your overall impressions of your Detective Bulletin Board. By the end of this chapter, you will have distilled the details down to key points and themes on your Business Landscape play sheet so you can easily refer back to the essential information.

EXERCISE

Create a Business Self-Portrait

Now we turn the spotlight back on you and your business. After all, you are part of the overall business landscape, too (one of the most important parts, I'd say!). Here you'll be creating a Business Self-Portrait by looking at your own strengths, challenges, and opportunities. Allow the following questions to spark your imagination:

- What is your background and experience?
- What are your special skills and talents?

Take a page out of marketing maven Rebecca Badger's book and ask your clients and colleagues for feedback about yourself to help you craft your Business Self-Portrait.

- How do you help your customers? What do they come to you for? What benefits do they receive?
- What products and/or services do you offer?
- What have your customers said about you and your work? What recurring themes do you notice? How might this relate to the legacy you want to leave or impact you want to have?
- What makes you stand out from the crowd?
- What opportunities do you see for yourself and your business?
- What challenges do you face?
- If your business were a person, what would this person be like? How would he or she dress? What words would describe this person's personality? Where would he or she live?
- What's your specialty?
- Where do you have a leg up on your peers? Where would you like to have a leg up? Are you competing on price, features, customization, quality, service, or other differentiating factors?
- What other brands evoke the kind of energy or spirit you're going for? The brands could be inside or outside your industry; the important thing is that they have the emotional impact you desire. What qualities do these brands have that you like?

Using what came up for you, have fun writing a narrative or a character sketch of your business, or painting, collaging, or mind-mapping your Business Self-Portrait.

Sometimes it can be hard to hold a mirror up to yourself, so why not ask for help from former and current customers? You can send these questions to them via email or in an online survey, or interview them over the phone or in person. Feel free to tailor the questions to your business. If you haven't had any customers yet, enlist a few trusted friends or colleagues.

Sample Interview Guide for Past and Current Clients

- Why did you hire me? What problem were you looking to solve, or what need were you trying to meet?
- What benefits did you receive from working with me?
- Did you consider other providers? If so, what was the deciding factor in choosing to work with or buy from me?

- What three words would you use to describe me and/or my work?
- What other products or services would you like to see me offer, and why?
- What else would you like to share?

Sample Interview Guide for Friends and Colleagues

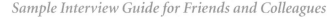

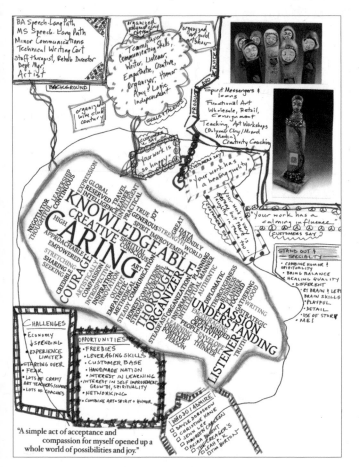

Mixed-media artist Amy Crawley mind-mapped her Business Self-Portrait and included images of her polymer clay sculptures, words to describe herself and notes from her self-reflection.

- What three words would you use to describe me?
- What would you say are my natural gifts, strengths, and passions?
- How do you think people can benefit from the gifts I have to offer?
- What could you see me happily doing as a creative/meaningful/authentic (use descriptors that feel appropriate to you) business? Please be as specific as you can.
- What else would you like to share?

Include the themes and insights you discover from these responses in your Business Self-Portrait. Once you're done, add your Business Self-Portrait to your Detective Bulletin Board, or have it nearby. Display your Big-Vision Collage from chapter 2 near the board as well.

Do a Gallery Walk

Now that you've enhanced your Detective Bulletin Board with some additional information about yourself, it's time to take a gallery walk. Take a few steps back from your board, and from any other related pieces you've made, so you can see everything as a whole. Imagine you are looking at a painting in a museum. What are your first impressions? What catches your eye? What patterns pop out at you? What might be a metaphor that represents the themes you see in your business landscape? What can you do more of, or less of? Where are the opportunities? What are you missing in your business?

Next, look over your Detective Bulletin Board and ask yourself questions that you might ask your perfect customer, such as: What is your emotional reaction to the business landscape? Where are you frustrated or angry because your needs aren't being met? In what instances are you satisfied by and comfortable with what's out there in the market? Jot down any notes from this initial pass.

Draw Your Conclusions

The Business Landscape play sheet shown at the beginning of the chapter on page 51 will help you synthesize the information you've gathered. Your business landscape lays the foundation for the other pieces of your Right-Brain Business Plan. It will help you make informed decisions about where to focus your time, resources, and dollars.

You'll be compiling the key points from the exercises you've done throughout this chapter and distilling them down to this one page. Also, feel free to draw your own landscape, as there might be different paths for your business, and the external market, that you want to explore.

Do a final gallery walk with the Business Landscape play sheet in hand. As you go, fill in the various sections on the play sheet to the best of your ability. You don't have to include a lot of detail — that's what your bulletin board was for. Instead, capture your overall impressions and highlight key points to inform the rest of your Right-Brain Business Plan. For fresh

Nicole Mason dreamed of creating a high-end floral design business that would serve up rustic and cosmopolitan beauty and style for small weddings and celebratory events. As Nicole painted the picture of her business landscape and made her Business Self-Portrait, she discovered opportunities to honor her personal values and strengths while aligning with eco-friendly trends and filling gaps in the marketplace. Her detective work revealed that she could set herself apart not only by providing gorgeous floral arrangements but also by focusing on locally grown, organic flowers, emphasizing her commitment to social responsibility, and giving back to the community. By staying true to her big vision and values, Nicole was inspired in a way that let her creative vision bloom.

Floral designer Nicole Mason played with colorful crayons, markers, and plenty of sparkles to create her dazzling "Glittery Flower Mama" Business Self-Portrait

perspectives, you could even invite a few friends or past clients to do the gallery walk with you. In addition to having them fill out the Business Landscape play sheet, have them reflect on big-picture questions and general observations such as the following:

- What are your initial impressions?
- What patterns or themes do you see?

Once these people have completed their gallery walks and jotted down their notes, start a discussion about what they discovered. You might want to designate someone as a note taker so you can focus on what is being shared.

Congratulations! You've just made it through one of the most arduous aspects of business planning. And I hope you had fun playing both detective and artist in the process. It's okay if your landscape still seems a bit out of focus, however; it'll get clearer as you go on. The important thing is that you got your ideas down on paper. Once you have information to work with, it's much easier to go back and test it out in the real world. Do your SWAGs need to be bigger or smaller? What might you have to offer your customers that will give you a leg up? You won't know how to make adjustments if you don't have a place to start from.

And so here you are, with your starting place. Next, you'll take the insights you've gained about your target market, your customers' needs, and what makes you stand out, and start developing your plan for getting the word out about yourself and your fabulous business.

- Prepare your Detective Bulletin Board and gather clues about your business landscape.
- Complete the Market and Trends play sheet.
- Organize and analyze the clues on your Detective Bulletin Board.
- Create a Business Self-Portrait.
- Conduct a gallery walk to discover patterns and themes.
- Fill out the Business Landscape play sheet.

LEFT-BRAIN CHECKLIST

Before moving on to the next chapter, review the checklist below. Your left brain will thank you!

- ❏ I have identified and described my target market, including my perfect customers' needs, as best I can for the time being.
- ❏ I have identified some hot trends that will affect my business.
- ❏ I have identified my direct and indirect competition.
- ❏ I have an idea of how I stand out from the crowd.
- ❏ I have identified some opportunities to get a leg up on my competition.

4 Getting the Word Out with Marketing

Find and Connect with Your Perfect Customers

When it comes to talking about your business, would you rather lay low than toot your own horn? Many right-brain entrepreneurs would rather let their creative work speak for itself than actively spread the word about what they do. Unfortunately, this means they limit their exposure to potential clients, which in turn can stunt the growth of their businesses. And that's definitely not what you want here, right?

You may be a rocking graphic designer or wedding photographer, or you may knit the most adorable wool hats, but if the right people don't know about the amazing work you have to offer, then how are they going to buy it? That's where a solid brand and brilliant marketing come in. These help you get the word out about your business in an intentional and targeted way. Even if you're already promoting your business, do you know what's working for you? Which of your marketing efforts are most effective? Are you spending too much money and not getting the results you want? Are you reaching the right people?

Time and again, I hear creative entrepreneurs confess that they avoid saying anything about their business because they haven't yet figured out exactly what to say. Well, guess what? The more you talk about your business, the more clarity you'll actually gain. Go figure! By sharing what you do, you'll see how people respond and you'll gather valuable feedback. Just like the process of planning a business, your marketing is an ongoing, always-changing effort, so give yourself permission to keep practicing.

LEFT-BRAIN CHILL PILL

Is your analytical mind telling you that you can't move a marketing muscle until you know exactly what to say? Relax. The more you practice articulating what you do, the clearer and easier the marketing will become.

For a good two to three painful years, I agonized over how to rebrand my coaching practice. I knew it wasn't the safe, corporate-looking brand I had originally come up with, but I wasn't quite sure how to infuse the creative, artistic elements that made what I had to offer unique. While I struggled to explain exactly what I did and how, each time I talked about my business I got to see what resonated with other people and with me. Eventually the pieces started to fall into place, and now I feel that my brand authentically represents me.

When you're clear about who you are and what your business stands for, it's much easier to communicate a clear message, even when you're not trying. Think of marketing as an enticing invitation to connect with your perfect customers. You started to get to know your perfect customers in the previous chapter as you explored your business landscape. In this chapter, you'll get to know your perfect customers in more detail as you step into their shoes, understand what makes them tick, and determine how best to reach them. You'll also identify your Getting the Word Out goals, select your preferred marketing mediums from a list of descriptions, and detail a Getting the Word Out plan, including your main messages and timing to get the word out.

What Is Marketing?

The American Marketing Association defines marketing as "the activity, set of institutions, and processes for creating, communicating, delivering, and exchanging offerings that have value for customers, clients, partners, and society at large."

In other words, it's how you let your perfect customers know that you have something they need. To get the word out, you'll need to define the overall goals you want to achieve with your marketing efforts, and develop a marketing plan that details the tactical steps to reach your perfect customers most effectively.

What Is Branding?

Your brand is the heart and soul of your business. It's the image, emotional response, and experience that comes to mind when people think of your business. A strong brand makes a consistent and lasting impression on your perfect customers and helps them remember who you are when it comes time to make the purchase. Your brand is the essence of what makes you stand out from the crowd. It shows up in what you say, how you say it, and who you say it to.

And it's more than just words. Your brand is also your tone, energy, and style. Whether you like it or not, you are a walking billboard. As a creative person, you probably already have a certain style in how you express yourself. Think about what words you would use to describe your personal

TIP

If you plan to use a branding consultant to help develop your brand image, or a graphic designer to create your logo, share your Right-Brain Business Plan with him even if it's not finished. In particular, he'll be curious about your Business Landscape play sheet, Business Self-Portrait, and Perfect Customer Portraits (we'll cover the latter in just a bit), which will give him a sense of your business and who you're targeting.

style or your company brand. Refer back to the Business Self-Portrait that you created in chapter 3 to help you articulate your brand. The more you can hone your brand, the more recognizable and memorable you'll be.

While a brand is the customer's intangible experience and perception of you, it also consists of tangible things, such as your company name, tagline, logo, and color palette. A strong brand lays the foundation for your marketing messages and mediums. For example, if you decided that your brand caters to upscale socialites who expect sophisticated quality, don't hand them black-and-white photocopied flyers. But if

Marketing consultant Rebecca Badger placed her collaged Right-Brain Business Plan pages in a spiral-bound photo album with a matching box, both in the same sunshine yellow she uses in her brand.

you're going after bargain hunters, they might appreciate the frugality of a ten-cent printout as opposed to a fancy full-color brochure that looks as if it cost an arm and a leg. Make sure your brand and marketing materials match your price point.

Clarify Your Getting the Word Out Goals

Before we jump into the specifics of how you want to reach your perfect customers, let's start by defining your marketing goals. What do you want to achieve by getting the word out about your business? Knowing what you ultimately want to get out of your marketing efforts will help you determine where to invest your time and money. Here are some examples of desired outcomes of successful marketing:

RIGHT-BRAIN BOOSTER

Pick a theme song for your brand or create a soundtrack for your business life. Play these tunes whenever you need inspiration.

- Earn fifty thousand dollars from new client projects by the end of the year
- Sell one hundred pieces, products, or packages during the holiday season
- Double your number of clients in the next three months
- Increase your brand recognition and exposure by getting twenty media placements in the next month
- Ramp up your mailing list by five hundred more subscribers in the next three months
- Have three hundred attendees at your event in September
- Land twenty-five new commissions by next quarter

Make sure you've identified at least one or two Getting the Word Out goals before creating your plan. That way your marketing activities will support your overall marketing goals. Write your goals in the first section of the Getting the Word Out play sheet as shown on the following page.

getting the word out!

My getting the word out goals:

1.

2.

The perfect customers I want to reach:

MARKETING MEDIUMS	MAIN MESSAGE	TIMING	RESOURCES NEEDED	ESTIMATED EXPENSES

PLAYSHEET

Who Are Your Perfect Customers?

When a portrait artist paints his subject, he takes time observing her. He takes in the subtle details of her face, notices the color and texture of her clothes, and attempts to capture the energy and essence she exudes. Look at defining your perfect customers with that same level of fascination and engagement. The more you know about your perfect customers, the easier it will be to connect with them.

Take a few moments to answer the following questions, even if you can't back up your general impressions with hard data. Refer back to people you've enjoyed working with in the past, and imagine others you'd want to work with in the future.

- Are your perfect customers male or female?
- How old are they?
- How much money do they make?
- What kind of education do they have?
- What kinds of jobs or careers do they have (or want to have)?
- Where do they live?
- What's their home-life situation? Are they single, married, divorced, or widowed? Do they have kids, have pets, and/or take care of their aging parents?
- What kinds of social and/or professional groups or organizations do they belong to, both in real life and online?
- Where do they shop?
- What do they spend their money on?
- Where do they get their information: from what specific TV shows, books, magazines, newspapers, websites, or blogs?
- How would you describe their personalities?

> **TIP**
>
> Guess what types of publications or magazines your perfect customers read. Visit those publications' websites and look at their advertising sections. They usually have a media kit section that includes some high-level demographics of their readership. Use these clues to infer more details about your perfect customers.

- What do they like or dislike?
- What do they do for fun?
- What lights them up?
- What do they value?
- What are their political views?

You may find that you have different groupings of your perfect customers. If that's the case, answer these questions for each group.

Once you have a sense of who you ideally want to work with, write a short description in the perfect customers section of the Getting the Word Out play sheet. You can also refine your description after going through the following perfect customer exercises.

Pen a heartfelt letter to your perfect customers, as Tori Deaux of the Circus Serene did with her love note to artists and writers.

Now that you've developed some sense of what makes your perfect customers tick, let's invite your right brain in to help paint the rest of the picture. You'll create visual profiles of each of your perfect customer groups to help you foster a more tangible connection with your audience. Through these images, you'll develop an intuitive sense of your perfect customers' energy, lifestyles, and motivations.

What you'll need:

- Magazines you think your perfect customers read
- Scissors
- Glue stick
- Large index cards (or other medium of your choice)

Instructions: Flip through magazines you think your potential clients might read. Find pictures of people who represent your perfect customers. Look for images that evoke their lifestyles. Cut out words or phrases that describe what they are like or what their needs are. Gather any leftover customer-related images from your Big-Vision Collage flipping-and-clipping. Group the images and words together and start gluing them to the fronts of the index cards. You can use any other visual medium you wish, such as large pieces of poster board or a page in your accordion book or journal. I like using index cards because they're easy to sort and to tuck away in the pockets or envelopes of my Right-Brain Business Plan. Plus, with the small surface area, your collage can be simple. It takes only a few images to capture the essence of your perfect customers.

If you have more than one group of perfect customers, create a separate collage for each.

On the back of each collaged card, jot down the qualities and attributes of your perfect customers. Use descriptions from the previous list of questions you reflected on.

Coach Amy Egenberger of Spirit Out!, Inc., helps people find inner strength, self-knowledge, and personal joy to energize their own creative journeys. By making her Perfect Customer Portraits, Amy discovered she loves working with two groups she defines as ARTpreneurs — "spirit-minded people who have a creative calling, inkling, or dream, and who are ready for help and learning to move forward" — and EDuCREAtors, "retired teachers who are spirit-based and longing to be of creative service in their lives 'after school.'" Having her perfect customer descriptions has made it much easier for Amy to talk about what she does and the clients she serves, and her visuals connect her to her deeper purpose.

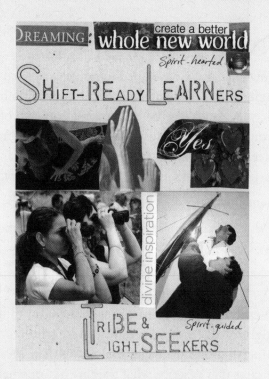

In addition to defining her target markets of ARTpreneurs and EDuCREAtors, coach and educator Amy Egenberger of Spirit Out!, Inc., also identified Shift-Ready Learners and Tribe and Light Seekers as her perfect customers.

EXERCISE

Write Character Sketches of Your Perfect Customers

Just as novelists and actors use character sketches to flesh out roles in a story, allow yourself to create a brief narrative about your perfect customer.

Compose a vignette describing a typical day in her life or write an anecdote that captures your perfect customer's essence. Ask yourself, how did she get to where she is now? Where does she want to go next? What matters to her? What are her biggest challenges, worries, or problems? Keep it simple and trust your intuition.

Sample Perfect Customer Character Sketch for a Career Coach

Sally is a success-oriented professional who climbed the corporate ladder for eight years. She has a college degree from a well-respected university and she's extremely intelligent and savvy. While she's achieved praiseworthy professional milestones, she feels burned-out and unsure of the path she's chosen. She fears that the cost of her success is the lack of balance and true passion in life. As a successful professional, she has the extra income to spend on self-help books, personal-growth workshops, and women's retreats. But while she's been devouring self-help resources like *O* magazine and *What Should I Do with My Life?* by Po Bronson on her morning train commutes, she feels that she isn't making progress fast enough. She's ready to invest in some focused, one-on-one support from a career coach, even though she's afraid to admit that she can't do it alone. She worries that if she doesn't act now, she'll just get trapped in the rat race.

Sample Perfect Customer Character Sketch for a Pet Portrait Photographer

My perfect set of customers is a young, upwardly mobile urban Bay Area couple starting their family by first adopting a dog. Rick and Jessica are passionate about their pooch, Jack. During the day while "Mom" and "Dad" work at their corporate jobs, their dog plays at a posh doggie day care. During the weekends, they take Jack to Fort Funston, where he loves to frolic with other pups along the beach. Valuing fun, adventure, and freedom, Rick and Jessica are active and like to be outdoors. They shop at REI, go to Tahoe to ski in the winter, and enjoy weekend getaways where their dog can tag along. They read *Wag* and *San Francisco* magazines. They have refined, modern tastes and decorate their home in the Marina District with pieces from West Elm and Crate and Barrel. Rick and Jessica want a fun, meaningful, and tasteful way to capture their favorite four-legged friend on film.

Sample Perfect Customer Character Sketch for a Recycled Clothing Designer

My perfect customer is someone like Allison, a twenty-something hipster who adores all things crafty and green. She values personal style and has a mission in life to be unique and to make a positive difference in the world. Her collection of one-of-a-kind handmade outfits and accessories reflects that. She supports independent artisans by purchasing much of her wardrobe and home decor from Etsy and at craft shows such as Crafty Bastards and Craft Renegade, or she buys used clothing at Goodwill and vintage stores. She wouldn't be caught dead in a department store or strip mall. She enjoys thumbing through magazines like *ReadyMade*, *Bust*, and *Boho* and browsing blogs such as decor8 and Design*Sponge. She enjoys her day job at a nonprofit, and on the weekends she can be found riding her bicycle to the local farmer's market with her silk-screened cloth tote bags in the basket.

EXERCISE

Role-Play with a Friend

Now that you've gained more clarity about your perfect customers, bring them to life by role-playing a conversation with them. Pick one of your Perfect Customer Portrait collages to start with. Use your right-brain imagination to step into your perfect customer's shoes. Get a friend to play a reporter who is interviewing you, the perfect customer. Your job is to imagine what it's like to live your perfect customer's life. Look back at what you jotted down in the customer needs section of your Business Landscape play sheet. Use the character sketch you wrote to help you craft a background story about what your perfect customer loves, hates, is challenged by, or needs help with. Have fun acting out what her frustrations would be. Use your voice and your whole body so you can have a visceral sense of what it feels like to live her life.

- What's your biggest frustration?
- What would help you?
- If your biggest frustration were addressed, what would that do for you? How would things be better?

Have your friend take notes on what you say. Then ask yourself the following:

- What did you notice when you were in the shoes of your perfect customer?
- What did you imagine that she felt, emotionally and physically?
- What need are you fulfilling for her when she buys your product or services?
- Now that you have a sense of what it may be like for her, what do you want her to know about how you can help her?

Using index cards and clippings from the favorite magazines of my target markets, I collaged Perfect Customer Portraits of professional women wanting more fulfillment, creative entrepreneurs, and moms in transition.

If you've read other business books or gone to networking meetings, you may have heard about elevator speeches or pitches. Basically, an elevator speech is a concise way of describing your business during the time it takes to ride a few floors in an elevator. The problem with a traditional elevator speech is that, by its very description, it's so one-way. With a speech or pitch, you're just talking at someone. But people don't want to be lectured to. When you use a right-brain approach that honors relationship, emotion, connection, and intuition, you move from a canned monologue to a meaningful dialogue with your perfect customer.

In a meaningful dialogue, you connect on an emotional level with the people you engage with. The interaction is two-way. You ask questions that show you are curious about what their needs are. These people in turn share their thoughts and ask you questions, too. Even if they are not your perfect customers, you've got an opportunity to describe what you do in a way that makes it easy for them to think of someone they know who needs what you provide. You should still be able to concisely describe what you do in a way that enrolls them. Use the right brain first to create an emotional connection and then to provide left-brain evidence to support your message.

Imagine that you're striking up a conversation with someone at a networking event or perhaps in a casual setting. Start by asking the person about himself. What does he do? What interests him? Your job is just to listen. What are you curious about? Get to know him. When it's your turn to share, simply say a little bit about yourself, including what you do and how you help people. You can have a short phrase that you use to describe your business, but weave it naturally into the conversation. Instead of selling, you are using your right-brain talents to connect and build a relationship. You might have a specific story to share about how you've helped someone in a situation similar to his.

This meaningful dialogue can also be used in various other formats to help you craft the main messages that you use in the marketing mediums you'll start choosing. Some of the main messages about your business that you should cover in your meaningful dialogue include the following:

- What you do (as you defined it in chapter 2)
- How you help people, or what problem your product or service solves (as you defined it in chapter 2)
- Who your perfect customers are (as you defined them in this chapter)
- What makes you unique (as you defined it in chapter 3)

The most important part of the meaningful dialogue is to be present and authentic. Most of the time, it's less about what you actually say and more about *how* you say it. It's how you show up that really engages people.

Choosing Your Marketing Mediums

You've done a great job of getting to know your perfect customers. Next, you'll need to decide how you're going to engage with them. You'll need to consider where they're most likely to show up and be receptive to your messages. Don't forget to also factor in what makes you most comfortable and successful when communicating. If you get energized while talking and mingling with people, you might want to consider attending networking events, speaking, being interviewed on TV, or demonstrating your techniques in person, versus sitting by yourself in front of your computer writing articles, blogging, or sending out an e-newsletter. If you're averse to a marketing medium you choose, either you'll end up finding every excuse in the book not to do it, or you'll begrudgingly do it and it will feel forced, to both you and your audience.

LEFT-BRAIN CHILL PILL

While there may be many marketing mediums mentioned, don't freak out. By no means do you need to use them all. Just pick a few to focus on that seem both fun and effective.

Next are descriptions of various marketing mediums, loosely categorized by how you might like to interact with people. You don't need to stick with one category or another; it's more a matter of honoring and balancing your energy. See which ones speak to you and your perfect customers. You'll want to mix and match marketing mediums and keep assessing whether they're working for you or not. Choose marketing mediums that will support the marketing goals you laid out at the beginning of the chapter.

Home Sweet Home

If you're the kind of entrepreneur who prefers to reach out to the rest of the world from the comfort of home (and your pj's), these writing- and graphic-based marketing activities may better suit your style.

- Send out a newsletter. A newsletter is a great way to establish regular communication with your perfect customers. What will you communicate? Will your newsletter include articles, tips, and inspiration, or information on events, shows, new offerings, and sales? Decide how often you want to send out your newsletter. Will it be monthly, weekly, or occasionally to promote upcoming events? What would meet the needs of your perfect customers? What will your perfect customers find of value? Consider offering a small freebie, such as a short e-book or download to entice subscribers. For example, if you're a knitter, offer a free basic pattern; or if you're a service professional, provide a free how-to report or a list of top ten tips. You can hold contests, challenges, or drawings, which encourage people to sign up for your mailing list. Who doesn't love to win prizes?

  While you can mail out a paper newsletter, electronic newsletters have many advantages. Online services allow you to track your subscriber statistics and run reports. Make sure your newsletter reflects your brand, and that you provide something of value. People are bombarded by so many marketing messages that yours needs to catch their eye and appeal to them.

- Write articles about subjects that your perfect customers care about. Getting published in magazines, on websites, and in blogs helps build your credibility as an expert in your field. Find blogs or websites where you can be a guest columnist or featured contributor. Think about what magazines your target audience reads, and see how you can get featured in them. For example, if your target audience is very spiritual, how can you get a story about yourself featured in magazines related to spirituality?

- Your own website or blog is a powerful marketing tool that lets you connect with your perfect customers. Through images, words, sound, video, and interactivity, you can convey much more than in print. A website is good for providing standard information about your company, including your products or services, your bio, your portfolio, and testimonials. A blog is good for sharing more timely information and for creating a more personal connection. On your blog you could give potential clients a peek into your life, your studio, or your company's activities. The great thing about a blog is that you can have a dialogue with people who leave comments. You get feedback on what resonates with people.

- Direct mail such as postcards or newsletters can be costly, but if you have a beautiful and memorable mailing item that is consistent with your brand, your perfect customers may be inspired to hang it up. Every

> **TIP**
>
> Start noticing what you find attractive in the marketing materials of other creative entrepreneurs or even other industries. Start a folder and collect advertisements, website pages, postcards, and other pieces that catch your eye. Or put these on your Detective Bulletin Board from chapter 3. Add sticky notes to each item and list exactly what it is that you like about it, such as colors, design, tone, messaging, size, or shape. Use these to kick-start your own ideas and inspirations.

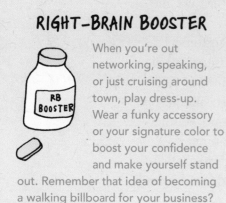
time they look at it, they'll be reminded of you.

- Colorful brochures with images and information are a great way to succinctly explain how you help people or what you're selling. Brochures are a good takeaway that convey more than a business card.

- Flyers are great for specific events or offerings such as a class, a show, or a sale. They are usually more time-sensitive than general brochures, are less costly, and require fewer design resources.

- Advertising is when you pay to get exposure. While this marketing method can cost a pretty penny, you benefit from having control of the ad's look and message. You can take out an ad in a local or national magazine or newspaper, pay to place your badge on someone's website or blog, sponsor an event, buy a radio or television spot, or bid on Internet keywords. Where might you want to advertise, and how much do you want to spend?

- With online social media, there are many options for connecting with people and customers. You can interact in real-time with people from around the world and get instant feedback, all without setting one foot outside your door. If community or connection is one of your values, social media are accessible platforms for building relationships and for helping your perfect customers get to know you.

Out and About

If you're the type of entrepreneur who loves to get spiffed up for a night on the town and to shine in the spotlight, here are some activities in the public eye that will be sure to get you out there.

- In-person networking can be really effective when you find events that draw your tribe. You might want to hang out with peers in your field to build relationships with potential strategic partners or people to refer to. Even if you're doing similar work, you may be the right contact for the next person they talk to. Or, you can find out where your perfect customers gather and connect with them there. Bring your business cards, but don't push them on everyone. Instead, hand them out to those you develop a relationship with, or as a way to follow up on a question you've asked or a resource you've provided to someone.

TIP

Remember that any interaction can be a form of networking (even talking to the cashier at the grocery store). You never know who others might know or what they might need. Chapter 6 has tips for cultivating new connections.

- Having a vendor table or booth at an event is another way to get more visible in your perfect customers' community. Venues could include art shows or fairs, community events, or trade shows and conferences for specific industries. With this option, there are other marketing and financial factors to consider. Booths can be costly at high-profile venues, and you might need to hire people to help you staff your booth. Also, the most effective booths create a brand experience, so you'll most likely need to have signage, displays, and other goodies to gussy up your space.
- Public speaking is a great way to get yourself out there and to practice having meaningful dialogues with your perfect customers on a larger scale. Speak at meetings of professional organizations, networking events, and conferences on a topic

that is of interest to your perfect customers; or give a demonstration of your work so that people get a firsthand experience of what you do. You can also consider teaching or leading workshops as a form of public speaking.

- Media such as podcasts, radio, and TV can help to increase your exposure and credibility. If you like being interviewed about what you do, this is a great marketing medium for you. You could hire a public relations agent to write a press release and help place you in newspapers and magazines and on radio and television shows. A PR agent can be expensive, so make sure you know how long you want to use an agent (maybe you have a new product coming out and want to promote it heavily for six months). This will help you budget for it, so you don't break the bank.

- There are also ways to do your own PR. You can sign up to get notified via email about different press inquiries. If you see a press inquiry that's relevant to your business, is on a subject you are an expert in, and would get you exposure to your perfect customers, then pitch your story or your quote directly to the contact person. Some PR listing services are free, or a perk, in certain networking organization memberships. I've suggested a PR inquiry listing service in the Resources section.

TIP

Once you start getting more press, consider creating an "in the news" or "press" section on your website or in your media kit to help build your credibility. Include links to where you've been featured in magazines or blogs, or on websites, TV, or radio.

Joining Forces

There are other marketing mediums where you actively partner with others to get the word out:

- Creative strategic alliances, which we'll cover in chapter 6, are a way to partner with complementary businesses to develop a new product or service or to simply help cross-promote each other.
- You can create a referral program by offering a special discount or gift to someone who refers a customer. Similarly, with an affiliate program, you can have other people selling your products or services; for every sale, they will earn a commission.
- Sales agents or sales representatives might be another way for you to gain exposure to and build business with your perfect customers, especially if some of those customers are other businesses. For example, an artist might hire a sales agent to help her get into high-end galleries. Or the creator of an inspirational greeting card line might hire a sales rep to sell the cards in bulk to gift and stationery stores.

Complete the Rest of Your Getting the Word Out Play Sheet

Next, finish filling out the detailed-plan section of your Getting the Word Out play sheet on page 78. Pick three to five marketing mediums to start with. As we talked about earlier, acknowledge your communication preferences and what you would really enjoy doing. For each marketing medium, jot down the main messages you want to get across. Do you have a sale or event that you want to promote? Are you launching a new program or product? How will these offerings help your perfect customers? Clearly state what's in it for them.

When Do You Want to Communicate What?

As you fill out the rest of the Getting the Word Out play sheet, consider the timing of your marketing activities. Think about how customers buy and when they buy. For instance, people looking for handmade holiday

Example of Completed Getting the Word Out Play Sheet

GETTING THE WORD OUT GOALS AND PLAN FOR A CRAFTER

My Getting the Word Out goals:

1. To sell $5,000 worth of merchandise at the fall craft fair
2. To get 20 new commissions by the end of November

The perfect customers I want to reach:

Young, creative women who enjoy handmade "green" goods and are shopping for themselves and for holiday gifts

Getting the Word Out Plan

MARKETING MEDIUMS	MAIN MESSAGES	TIMING	RESOURCES NEEDED	ESTIMATED EXPENSES
Postcard campaign	Announce upcoming craft show	Send out by September 1	Graphic designer to design postcard	$200 for graphic designer, $95 for printing 500 postcards, $140 for postage
Have a vendor booth at fall craft fair	Show fall jewelry line, special sales Special discount on e-book for the next two months	November 1	Volunteers to help at booth	$200 to rent a booth, $50 for signage
Get featured in local paper	Handmade gifts are popular; supporting local artisans is good for the city's economy; my jewelry includes recycled items gathered from the local area	October 15	Write a press release	None

gifts typically flock to craft fairs in November and December, so an artisan may consider renting space at a few seasonal craft shows during those months. Also, the beginning of the year is usually rife with folks eager to make good on their New Year's resolutions, so that might be a great time for a life coach, personal trainer, or holistic health counselor to announce a new goal-setting program.

Proactively scheduling your marketing activities can help you align with your perfect customers' needs. It also helps you stay focused and encourages you to distribute your efforts and resources throughout the year. You may want to do smaller, less expensive marketing in the months before you invest in a broader marketing campaign like a big expo or a lengthy media tour around the country.

Marketing campaigns are discrete marketing efforts that have a beginning and an end. For example, you might create a marketing campaign to gear up for a future show. Or you might be running a holiday sale for a limited time. In contrast, a standard website or brochure is a general, ongoing marketing component that sustains your brand.

Resources and Support Needed

What kind of help might you need for your marketing activities? Do you need to hire a website designer or an expert to set up your blog? Do you need to work with a PR agent? How much do you estimate this will cost? These are just some questions to get you thinking about other people you might need to involve. We'll cover this in more detail in chapter 6.

Costs of Marketing

While some things, like word of mouth and social media, can be free, many marketing mediums cost money. You need to spend money to make money, so think of it as an investment. Determine how much your chosen marketing mediums will cost. For example, how much will it be to make flyers or use an e-newsletter service? What do you guess your competitors might be spending on their marketing? What marketing tactics are they using? What's your sense of what works for them? And why? How might this help you? In the next chapter, we'll look at the overall finances in more detail. This is just to get you thinking about it.

Example of Completed Getting the Word Out Play Sheet

GETTING THE WORD OUT GOALS AND PLAN FOR A COACH

My Getting the Word Out goals:

1. To sell 100 e-books in the next two months
2. To get two new clients by April 1

The perfect customers I want to reach:

Creative, professional, and entrepreneurial women between the ages of 25 and 50 who want more fulfillment, meaning, and balance in their life

Getting the Word Out Plan

MARKETING MEDIUMS	MAIN MESSAGES	TIMING	RESOURCES NEEDED	ESTIMATED EXPENSES
Newsletter	Inspiring stories, tips, announcements	2nd Tuesday of each month	Email campaign service	$20/month
Guest blog posts	Tips on balance, creativity, and life purpose	Monthly	Identify websites	None
Advertise on targeted blogs	Special discount on e-book for the next two months	Monthly	Hire graphic designer to design ad, research which blogs would reach my perfect customers	$200 for graphic designer, $150/month for running ads

Mix It Up

You'll find that marketing involves a lot of trial and error. Allow yourself to experiment and see what works for you. If you already use certain marketing mediums, consider adding new ones that will reach your target market from a different direction. The more that people see your name and brand, the easier it will be to recognize you, recall you, and buy from you.

Make Sure You Seal the Deal

Now that your beautifully enticing marketing materials have convinced your perfect customers that they must have what you offer, don't forget to actually make the sale! The sale is the point where money changes hands. Just because people have told you how much they adore your gorgeous handcrafted jewelry or how they desperately want to hire you as their graphic designer, they are not paying customers until they actually buy from you. Your business won't earn a dime from words of interest alone. The sale bridges the gap between marketing and making the moola. Knowing how you're going to handle sales will make it easier to get from compliments to cash. How will you accept payment? Will it be cash and check only? Will you set up a merchant account so you can accept credit cards in person and/or online? Will you offer payment plans? We'll go into this further when we discuss the operational plan in chapter 8, but it's important to start thinking about it now, before we head into the next chapter, on finances.

- Create your Perfect Customer Portraits.
- Write character sketches for your perfect customers.
- Engage in a meaningful dialogue with your perfect customers.
- Define your Getting the Word Out goals and plan.

LEFT-BRAIN CHECKLIST

Before moving on to the next chapter, review the checklist below. Your left brain will thank you!

❏ I can describe my perfect customers, and I know where to find them.

❏ I have developed or started to develop my brand.

❏ I have identified my Getting the Word Out goals.

❏ I have identified my top three to five marketing mediums and have outlined the main messages, timing, and resources needed in my Getting the Word Out play sheet.

❏ I have determined how I will receive payment.

5 Managing the Moola — Color by Numbers

Develop a Financial Plan with Fun and Flair

Well, my right-brained friends, let's be honest; we're at the point in the process where creatives might suddenly feel an urgent need to do laundry, walk the dog, or take a nice long nap. Yep, you guessed it. We're headed into the dreaded numbers! But wait; don't go running for the hills. Sure, the financial part of the business plan can seem scary and intimidating to many of us. However, one of the most thrilling and rewarding aspects of running your own business is making a living doing what you love. Instead of passively receiving a paycheck from a soul-sucking rat-race job, you get to feel the pride of turning your creative passion into profit and to appreciate every hard-earned dollar. Now, that's something to stick around for and get excited about. So, let's talk more about bringing home the bacon. I swear it won't be as yucky as you think!

You'll be surprised to know that your right brain is actually an asset when it comes to your finances. Your left brain will help you pinpoint your specific expenses, but your right brain will be able to discover the bigger picture and patterns, especially when you use visual aids. Plus, your right brain sees past the numbers to connect with how your earnings can help you honor your values in work and other aspects of your life. Your right brain knows that your creative business is not just about making money — it's also about finding meaning and enjoyment in pursuing your passions.

Despite how daunting the numbers might seem, it's important to have a clear sense of how you're managing the moola. In the simplest terms, you'll need to know how you're making money and how to make more, as well as how you're losing money and how to lose less.

This chapter will empower you to develop a visual financial plan with fun and flair. You'll learn some basic financial terms, you'll play with pricing, and you'll set some high-level financial goals. You don't have to become a financial whiz or an accounting expert, by any stretch of the imagination. I know that's not why you picked up this book! When it comes to finances, let's move from fear and frustration to focus and flow.

While you'll want to have a basic understanding of the numbers, there are many financial experts out there who help business owners make sense of their dollars and cents. You can partner with a professional, such as a tax accountant, bookkeeper, or financial planner, for in-depth guidance or patient handholding. Just like you love being creative, they love working with numbers (thank goodness!). Chapter 6 will help you create your support team, including your left-brain counterparts.

LEFT-BRAIN CHILL PILL

Your judging, logical mind loves to make up rules (and man, don't even get it started on rules about money and worth!). If you have old rules that are no longer serving you, you have full permission to let them go. Burn them. Flush them down the toilet.

This Managing the Moola page from artist Amy Crawley's visual plan is a great reminder to embrace abundance as you define your financial goals.

Releasing Mental Money-Baggage

At the heart of it, money, or currency, is an exchange of energy. Before we dive into the numbers, it's important to explore what helps or hurts this flow of energy for you. Many right-brain entrepreneurs have mental baggage that holds them back when it comes to money, numbers, wealth, and abundance. Let's look at some common limiting beliefs to see what might be getting in the way of maximizing your financial success.

I hate math, and/or I'm not a numbers person. Believe me, as someone whose worst grades were always in math, I totally get the feeling that numbers just aren't for you. Fortunately, the work in this chapter calls for only very basic arithmetic — adding, subtracting, multiplying, and dividing — which I know you are fully capable of doing; and most tools and financial systems will handle that for you anyway. There won't be talk of cosines or statistics here. In fact, the most challenging thing will be for you to come up with the numbers to plug in. But that just takes a bit of research, asking around, and, you guessed it, some creative guessing that happens to be more art than science. It's really the psychological barrier that gets people, rather than the actual math.

I don't want to become a sellout./Money is evil. Creative types often worry that they'll sell themselves out if they make money doing their art. They fear they'll lose their artistic integrity or creative edge if they become too commercial, so they stay with the starving artist stereotype and wonder why it's such a struggle to make ends meet. As an artist and creative soul, you have something special that you're offering the world, and you deserve to make an honest living from your contribution.

I'd rather just give my work away for free. Similarly, people who live for making a positive difference can keep themselves in martyr mode by volunteering their work too much or never charging enough. Driven by a strong sense of altruism, you may feel awkward or selfish accepting payment for sharing your natural gifts. But if you're really in business for yourself, you do need to earn a living, so let's find a way for you to be generous to others while also being generous to yourself. The more you value yourself, the more others will value you.

It's hard to make money. Yes, bringing home the bacon requires some blood, sweat, and tears. But you don't have to kill yourself to make a living. It's hard to make money when you don't have any idea about what's working and what's not. Understanding your finances will enable you to make money more easily.

I don't have enough money to get started or to grow my business. Sometimes people get stuck thinking they can't move forward without funding. That may be true to a certain extent, especially if you're looking at the ultimate vision of your business. But don't let that stop you from starting. What's the minimum investment you need to take the next step? Start small to get big!

You might relate to some of the limiting beliefs mentioned, or you might have your own slew of broken records playing in your head. Regardless, I bet you are way more capable of dealing with finances than you give yourself credit for. Don't get trapped by your excuses and fears. When you stick with the basics, managing the moola isn't as difficult as you may think it is. It can be a relatively simple process having just a few steps. And when you take a right-brain approach, you might even crack a smile.

Professional organizer and concierge Beth DeZiel included a lucky dollar on her wealth and abundance vision board (close-up shown here) to remind her that money is simply an exchange of energy.

 **RIGHT-BRAIN REFLECTION**

What are your limiting beliefs when it comes to money or abundance? Even if you've explored this inquiry before, be honest with yourself. Are you 100 percent satisfied with your financial situation? If not, what's holding you back?

Write your answers to the Right-Brain Reflection questions on a sheet of paper. For example, you might write down: "Money is hard to make," "I'm doing this for the love of my art, so making money feels wrong," or "The numbers are too hard to understand." Notice the sensations in your body as you articulate whatever it is that holds you back. If you feel constricted or tense, note the place in your body where you sense this most strongly and simply be aware of any emotions you may have.

Next, on a separate piece of paper, reframe those old limiting beliefs into new, positive, empowering statements. For example, if you wrote, "Money is hard to make," change it to something meaningful and inspiring, like: "It's easy to make money, because my perfect clients love paying me for my work." Or: "I enjoy making money by providing a valuable service that makes a difference." Also, reconnect to the vision of wealth and abundance you saw for yourself in chapter 2. See where wealth and abundance showed up for you on your Big-Vision Collage. What other new, positive statements will support that vision? When you connect with these statements, notice how you feel in your body. What's different now?

Then take the piece of paper with your limiting beliefs written on it, crumple it, tear it up, burn it, or throw it in the trash. Those beliefs are no longer serving you. Feel free to create your own releasing ritual to let go of your mental money-baggage. I once had a client who flushed her list of limiting beliefs down the toilet, and she sure had a blast doing it!

Return to your positive statements and read them aloud. You might even want to stand up and hold your arms wide open, ready to receive abundance. Let these affirmations resonate throughout your body. Repeat them back to yourself whenever you find yourself getting stuck when it comes to money. Have your written affirmations visible while you're working on your Right-Brain Business Plan to keep you connected with thoughts of abundance and empowerment.

Ringmaster Tori Deaux of the Circus Serene tamed her financial fears by writing what she calls "wild-ass happy" estimates on her playful Managing the Moola plan.

Getting a Clear (or at Least Clear-ish) Financial Picture

It's helpful to get a rough baseline of your financial picture when you're starting to manage the moola. Answer the following questions as best you can. You can look at receipts or bank statements to help you piece together the picture, or you can just make a ballpark estimate.

- How much did you spend last year on your business? (Expenses.)

LEFT-BRAIN CHILL PILL

LB

If you're going cross-eyed or want to pull your hair out while trying to answer these questions, connect with your affirmations and breathe.

TIP

The following Moola Map exercise will help you make educated guesses as you answer the first two questions. Just getting numbers to start with can be one of the hardest parts of figuring out your finances. Be gentle and patient with yourself. The more you gradually chip away at this, the more information you'll have to work with, and, over time, this will make managing the moola much easier. The point is, you gotta start somewhere, so start here.

- How much did you make in sales last year in your business? (Income.)
- How much did you make in profit? (Income minus expenses.)
- How much money do you need to cover personal expenses? (This will give you a sense of how much you will need to pay yourself.)
- How much cash do you currently have available in your business?

EXERCISE

Make Your Moola Map

Begin getting a handle on your financial picture by identifying your income and expenses. You may be expecting me to tell you to crack open a spreadsheet, but don't worry; we're going to do something much more inviting than that. When we do this exercise in my workshops, participants let out a big sigh of relief as they discover they get to play with colors and move items around with their hands. So let's get a visual inventory of where your money comes in (income/sales) and goes out (expenses/costs) by making your Moola Map.

What you'll need:

- Sticky notes (pink and green, or two other colors)
- Colored markers (red, green, and black)
- Large piece of paper or flipchart paper
- Masking tape
- Some wall space or a large working area

Moola Map

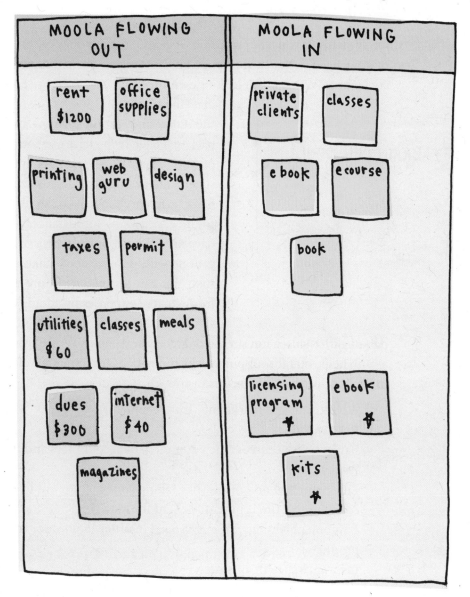

MOOLA FLOWING OUT

- rent $1200
- office supplies
- printing
- web guru
- design
- taxes
- permit
- utilities $60
- classes
- meals
- dues $300
- internet $40
- magazines

MOOLA FLOWING IN

- private clients
- classes
- e book
- ecourse
- book
- licensing program ✻
- e book ✻
- kits ✻

Instructions: Tape the large piece of paper to the wall. Draw a vertical line down the middle of the paper with your black marker. At the top of the left column write: "Moola flowing out" or "What I spend money on"; and at the top of the right-hand column write: "Moola flowing in" or "What I make money on."

Moola Flowing Out: Your Expenses

On the left side you'll be capturing what you spend money on. Off the top of your head, write each of your business expenses on a separate pink sticky note. When possible, jot down the exact cost; otherwise, guessti-mate the amount by month or year, or leave the dollar amount off for now and come back to it later. If you have previous records of your expenses — past receipts, bank statements, or a bookkeeping system — feel free to reference those. If you think of some future expenses — for instance, you don't have an office yet but you believe you will get one within the year — make a note of that. You can distinguish future expenses from current expenses by adding a dot or star in the corner of the sticky note (or a dab of glitter glue, a fun sticker, or any other delightful embellishment).

LEFT-BRAIN CHILL PILL

I know the list of expenses may seem long and overwhelming, but don't worry. These expenses may not all apply to you; just focus on the ones that relate to you and your business.

To help you fill your pink sticky notes, here are some typical expense categories for small businesses:

- Advertising and marketing (from chapter 4)
- Auto expenses
- Bank service charges (such as merchant account fees and PayPal fees)
- Entertainment and meals (like taking your mentor out to coffee or meeting a potential client for lunch)
- Equipment (things you might need in order to produce your products)
- Insurance (health, business, etc.)

- Internet hosting
- Legal fees
- Licenses and permits
- Membership dues (for your professional networks)
- Office furniture
- Office supplies
- Postage
- Printing
- Professional fees (for your bookkeeper, designer, coach, agent, or others who may be identified in chapters 4 and 6)
- Rent (office, studio, or storage space)
- Sales tax (if you sell tangible goods, collect sales tax directly from your customers and then pay it to the state government at regular intervals)
- Software
- Subscriptions (magazines, newspapers, websites)
- Supplies or raw materials for producing your goods
- Training/classes/education (any workshops or classes you might need to take to gain new skills)
- Travel expenses
- Utilities
- Salary paid to you (how much you will pay yourself)
- Salary paid to any employees
- Income taxes (you'll need to estimate, or ask your accountant)

List everything you can think of on your sticky notes. You may not know the actual numbers yet, and that's okay. Once you have all your expense sticky notes up, you can start organizing them by amount from biggest to smallest to make more sense of your financial picture.

Moola Flowing In: Your Income

On the right side of the page, you'll be capturing all the ways you make money. Off the top of your head, write each moola-making method in your business on a separate green sticky note. If you know your actual sales numbers from last year, include those, or guesstimate. Capture your existing income sources, like the products and services you currently sell. Plus, dream up ideas for other ways to make money down the road. As you write moola-making methods on the sticky notes, be as broad or as narrow as you want to be. For example, if you're a jeweler, you may want to have general product categories — such as "necklaces, earrings, and bracelets" — instead of having a sticky note for each specific style you make. And if you also make custom pieces and teach jewelry-making workshops, you'll want to capture those additional income streams on separate sticky notes, too. This will help you see where most of your money comes from. For ideas about future income, just put a dot or star on the corner of the sticky note to differentiate it from your existing income sources. For more ideas about what to write on the green sticky notes, read the next section.

Once you have written all your green sticky notes, you can do the additional step of starting to group them together in ways that make sense to you. For example, perhaps certain items are related or can be packaged together in new ways. Maybe you could organize them from biggest earner to least profitable, or by current offerings and future offerings. Use your right brain to help you see patterns and the bigger picture.

More Ways to Have Moola Flowing In

You did a great job identifying income opportunities in the previous exercise. Let's continue brainstorming additional moola-making methods. Reflect back to your Big-Vision Visualization from chapter 2 and remember how it felt to imagine living with abundance — what it was like to envision people happily paying you money again and again. What other products or services could they pay you for? Look back at your Big-Vision Collage to see if that sparks a few more moola-making methods. If you need ideas for more ways to bring home the bacon, the following are some basic models for making money.

Active Moola-Making Methods

With active moola-making methods, you've got your hands busily and directly in your work in order to generate income in exchange for the time it takes to provide your services or make your goods.

Money for time. If you're a service-based business, like a counselor, coach, massage therapist, personal trainer, graphic designer, or consultant, you most likely charge by the hour for one-on-one sessions with your clients. In this scenario, you make money only while you're providing your service. You could create packages for your services so that your perfect customers buy a discounted series. They'd catch a break, and you'd ensure a steadier flow of income. To get more bang for your money-for-time buck, consider offering services such as workshops, courses, events, or group sessions that allow you to reach more people and bring in more money for the same amount of your time.

Money for goods. If you're selling products or tangible goods, you'll probably charge by the item or by groupings of items. You'll need to factor in the cost of making your goods, whether handmade or manufactured, in order to make a profit. Take a look at the pricing section for more suggestions on how to determine pricing. If you're selling handmade pieces, perhaps you charge more because of their unique artisanal quality. If you want to limit the time you spend making things, you could explore the possibility of manufacturing your items or outsourcing production.

Commissioned work. If you're an artist or crafter, you can offer, in addition to the readymade goods you keep in stock, personalized pieces on commission. Usually these are priced at a premium because you are making a one-of-a-kind object for your customer.

Passive Moola-Making Methods

With passive moola-making methods, you may have your hands in the work upfront, but once that initial time and effort are invested, you can reap the benefits almost without lifting a finger. In some passive moola-making methods, you don't have your hands in the work at all.

Licensing. Artists, graphic designers, photographers, writers, or content creators might consider licensing their work. You invest your money and time once to create a piece or product that you give other companies the right to reproduce or repurpose; you receive a residual income from that.

Affiliates. You create a product, and people who sell your product get a cut. You expand your reach by tapping into your affiliates' networks, and you help other entrepreneurs make additional income, too. You could also become an affiliate of another company whose products you believe in, and earn a commission.

Subscription, membership, or monthly fee. For some businesses, such as yoga studios, art centers, networking organizations, or online community sites, it might make sense to charge customers an ongoing fee.

There are many other innovative income streams and creative business models out there. Here's another chance for you to use your intuitive right brain to see the patterns and big-picture opportunities. You get to be creative about how you'll bring in money. What combinations might you consider to maximize your moola? Mix and match to create a prosperous patchwork that works for you and your business. On green sticky notes, jot down any of these ideas that you want to pursue and place them on the right side of your Moola Map.

Doing a Moola Map Values Check

After you've noted all your expenses on the pink sticky notes, and your income on the green sticky notes, take a step back, review your Moola

SUCCESS STORY

After developing her first Right-Brain Business Plan, Rena Tucker landed several high-paying portrait commissions. She also explored other moola-making methods, such as cartooning and offering online classes. Despite her financial success, Rena felt burned-out and unsatisfied. Something needed to change. By reconnecting to her creative muse, Rena found the courage to leave her successful art business so she could follow her new passion. She cofounded U.S.A. Mercantile Corp., a jewelry and apparel company that believes in "making it cool again to be an American." Rena's latest Right-Brain Business Plan depicts her muse, "Renalbert" (a play on Jill Badonsky's muse Albert from the book *The Nine Modern Day Muses and a Bodyguard*), and U.S.A. Mercantile Corp.'s official spokesmodel, Annie, a mannequin, donning some of the company's wares. Rena's bold move reminds us that it's important to reap both financial and emotional rewards from our business.

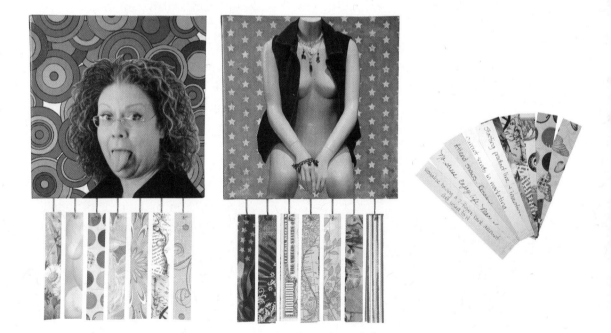

Creative entrepreneur Rena Tucker of U.S.A. Mercantile Corp. noted her financial goals, values, affirmations, and actions on the back of decorative strips of paper that hang from her irreverent visual plan.

Map, and do a quick values check. Connect back with the values you identified in chapter 2. How do your values relate to the moola-making methods you have now? If you aren't currently honoring your values, what can you do to honor them? For example, let's say you value freedom, but all you have is money-for-time pink sticky notes. Then the only way to make more money is to work more hours. However, that may not align well with your freedom value, especially because there are only so many hours in a day. Based on your values check, make any necessary adjustments to your Moola Map to ensure that your business makes your heart sing.

Taking It a Step Further: Plugging in the Numbers

To get a more accurate read on your Moola Map, the next step is to take each of the sticky note items and enter them into the Rid the Red, Grow the Green spreadsheet (visit Rightbrainbusinessplan.com to download the template). The good news is, you've done a lot of the legwork already, and it's just a matter of plugging in the numbers.

In the top section of the spreadsheet, enter all your green sticky notes under the subhead "How much moola will I bring in?" This is where you include your projected income from all of your products and services. In the bottom section, enter all your pink sticky notes under the subhead "How much moola will I spend?" You may need to update the names of the categories based on what you created in your Moola Map. Also, don't forget to pay yourself a salary, if you can swing it.

You'll notice that there is a column for the year and a column for each month. It's helpful to project how much you'll make from each product or service every month. You

RIGHT-BRAIN BOOSTER

If spreadsheets make you want to scream, then by all means, scream! Find a private place to shout into a pillow. Yell and shake your fists. Rather than keeping the frustration pent up inside, let the feelings flow through you until they dissipate. It's quite cathartic. And, yes, I'm speaking from personal experience here.

can base your projection on the natural cycles of your business; for example, crafters might predict an increase in sales in October, November, and December because their perfect customers buy gifts for the holidays. Or you might plan on launching a new offering in the middle of the year, so you can anticipate a spike in sales during your promotion time. The same goes for projecting your spending. You can do it by month, or you can just enter the total for the year. The benefit of breaking down your income and expenses by month is that you can see where you might need to make adjustments in your timing or schedule.

Once you plug in all the numbers from your Moola Map, the downloaded spreadsheet (which has formulas in it) will automagically do the calculations for you, and you'll be able to see your profit (your income minus your expenses). If the numbers show up in the red, then you're losing money. You want to rid the red to grow the green — and make a profit.

Example of Completed Rid the Red, Grow the Green Spreadsheet

Rid the Red, Grow the Green: A Very, Very Basic Look at My Finances
Some left-brain details for my Right-Brain Business Plan

	For the Year	January	February	March	April	May	June	July	August	September	October	November	December
How much moola will I bring in?													
Income, or moola flowing in													
Original art	$11,250	$500	$500	$500	$500	$500	$500	$500	$750	$1,000	$1,000	$2,500	$2,500
Commissioned work	$28,000	$2,000	$2,000	$2,000	$2,000	$2,000	$2,000	$3,000	$2,000	$2,000	$2,000	$2,000	$5,000
Art prints, cards, calendars	$3,600	$300	$300	$300	$300	$300	$300	$300	$300	$300	$300	$300	$300
Creativity e-course	$5,400	$450	$450	$450	$450	$450	$450	$450	$450	$450	$450	$450	$450
Five-day retreat	$3,000	$0	$0	$0	$3,000	$0	$0	$0	$0	$0	$0	$0	$0
Art workshop	$5,250	$750	$0	$750	$0	$750	$750	$0	$750	$750	$750	$0	$0
Total income	$56,500	$4,000	$3,250	$4,000	$6,250	$4,000	$4,000	$4,250	$4,250	$4,500	$4,500	$5,250	$8,250
How much moola will I spend?													
Expenses, or moola flowing out													
Advertising	$900	$300	$0	$300	$0	$0	$0	$0	$0	$300	$0	$0	$0
Auto expenses	$160	$20	$0	$20	$20	$20	$20	$0	$20	$20	$20	$0	$0
Bank service charges	$60	$5	$5	$5	$5	$5	$5	$5	$5	$5	$5	$5	$5
Entertainment and meals	$200	$0	$0	$0	$0	$0	$0	$0	$0	$200	$0	$0	$0
Equipment	$0	$0	$0	$0	$0	$0	$0	$0	$0	$0	$0	$0	$0
Insurance	$300	$0	$0	$300	$0	$0	$0	$0	$0	$0	$0	$0	$0
Internet hosting	$120	$10	$10	$10	$10	$10	$10	$10	$10	$10	$10	$10	$10
Legal fees	$300	$0	$0	$300	$0	$0	$0	$0	$0	$0	$0	$0	$0
Licenses and permits	$50	$50	$0	$0	$0	$0	$0	$0	$0	$0	$0	$0	$0
Membership dues	$0	$0	$0	$0	$0	$0	$0	$0	$0	$0	$0	$0	$0
Office furniture	$0	$0	$0	$0	$0	$0	$0	$0	$0	$0	$0	$0	$0
Office supplies	$200	$50	$0	$0	$50	$0	$0	$50	$0	$0	$50	$0	$0
Postage	$240	$20	$20	$20	$20	$20	$20	$20	$20	$20	$20	$20	$20
Printing	$200	$0	$0	$0	$0	$0	$0	$0	$0	$200	$0	$0	$0
Professional fees (accounting, design, coaching, etc.)	$1,000	$0	$0	$500	$0	$0	$500	$0	$0	$0	$0	$0	$0
Rent, office	$0	$0	$0	$0	$0	$0	$0	$0	$0	$0	$0	$0	$0
Sales tax	$675	$30	$30	$30	$30	$30	$30	$30	$45	$60	$60	$150	$150
Software	$0	$0	$0	$0	$0	$0	$0	$0	$0	$0	$0	$0	$0
Subscriptions	$0	$0	$0	$0	$0	$0	$0	$0	$0	$0	$0	$0	$0
Supplies or raw materials for producing goods	$1,800	$250	$0	$250	$0	$250	$0	$350	$0	$350	$0	$350	$0
Training/classes/education	$0	$0	$0	$0	$0	$0	$0	$0	$0	$0	$0	$0	$0
Travel expenses	$1,500	$0	$0	$0	$500	$0	$0	$0	$0	$1,000	$0	$0	$0
Utilities	$600	$50	$50	$50	$50	$50	$50	$50	$50	$50	$50	$50	$50
How much will I pay myself? (Salary)	$36,000	$3,000	$3,000	$3,000	$3,000	$3,000	$3,000	$3,000	$3,000	$3,000	$3,000	$3,000	$3,000
Total expenses	$44,305	$785	$115	$1,785	$685	$385	$635	$515	$150	$2,215	$215	$585	$235
Total income minus total expenses	$12,195	$3,215	$3,135	$2,215	$5,565	$3,615	$3,365	$3,735	$4,100	$2,285	$4,285	$4,665	$8,015
Income taxes	$4,878	$0	$0	$0	$1,220	$0	$1,220	$0	$0	$1,220	$0	$0	$1,220
Bringing home the bacon (Profit)	$7,317	$3,215	$3,135	$996	$4,346	$3,615	$2,146	$3,735	$4,100	$1,066	$4,285	$4,665	$6,796

Some Basic Financial Terms

While we won't get into a whole lot of detail while discussing these terms, it's good for you to have a basic sense of the lingo, especially if you'll be working with an accountant, a bank loan officer, or investors. And, as if the jargon wasn't confusing enough already, note that some of the terms also have alternative names, but they still mean exactly the same thing.

- *Income (or sales, total income, gross income, total sales, gross sales, revenue, earnings, or total earnings).* Your business's total sales over a period of time, or in simpler terms, the money coming into your business.

- *Expenses (or costs).* What you spend money on to run your business, or in other words, the money going out. Your expenses could be fixed expenses, which are the same amount each month (such as rent or a standing monthly membership fee) or variable expenses, which can change over time (such as your phone bill or fees paid to your graphic designer).

- *Profit (or net income).* Your income, minus expenses. Basically, profit is what you want to have: money left over after you pay your expenses, including, remember, a salary for yourself.

- *Profit and loss statement (or profit and loss sheet, P&L, P&L sheet, P&L statement, or income statement).* Shows your income, expenses, and profit over a period of time, including a projection into the future. It gives you a snapshot of your business's ability to make money. (The Rid the Red, Grow the Green spreadsheet is a very basic right-brain version of a profit and loss statement.)

- *Balance sheet.* Shows your company's assets (things of value that you own, like your computer or other equipment) and liabilities (where the money came from to pay for those assets) — in other words, what you own and what you owe. This shows how healthy your business is, and banks like to see healthy companies when they're considering loans.

- *Cash flow statement.* Shows money coming in and money going out over a period of time. It's important to pay attention to your cash flow, because — even if you're bringing in a lot of money — when you need to pay your expenses before your customers pay you, your well might run dry.

- *Profit margin.* The percentage of profits you earn from your sales. For example, if you sold an art piece for a thousand dollars, and it cost you two hundred dollars to make the item, you would have eight hundred dollars in profit, and your profit margin would be 80 percent.

- *Cost of goods sold (also called by its acronym, COGS).* The cost of buying your raw materials or supplies, plus the cost of labor to make the finished, tangible products that you sell to your customers. Usually COGS is captured in a detailed profit and loss statement.

How Will You Price Your Products or Services?

As you play with the numbers to find the sweet spot for yourself and your perfect customers, you'll probably discover that what you charge your customers for your work can be more art than science. There isn't one magic formula for pricing. Since each business has its own mix of products and services, financial goals, perfect customers, operations, and other variables that factor into the pricing, we'll cover basic philosophies and approaches here.

There are two common approaches to figuring out what you'll charge: covering your costs and maximizing the perceived value of your services or goods. At the bottom end of the spectrum, you can base your price on

LEFT-BRAIN CHILL PILL

If you're worried about whether you'll make enough dough doing what you love, take a moment to breathe. I know it can be difficult to take a hard look at the moola, so, first off, bravo to you for being willing to explore what's working and not working. Remember, it's common to be in the red or to just break even when you're starting out. Transform the discouragement into curiosity and look for creative ways to bring in more moola.

costs (such as materials and labor) to make sure you cover your expenses and make a profit. At the top end, you can experiment with pricing based on what you think people are willing to spend. If you can get top dollar because your perceived value and quality support a big price tag, then great. If not, you'll probably land somewhere in the area between covering costs and perceived value.

Once you're done fiddling with the numbers, see how your price tag stacks up against what others in your field are charging. Flip back to the business landscape work you did in chapter 3 to see where you fit in with your peers. Are you at the high end, middle, or low end of the price range? Does that align with where you'd expect to find your perfect customers? Ultimately, you have to do what feels right to you in terms of your own expenses and the value of your services or products, and you'll need to find perfect customers willing to pay that.

Visit Rightbrainbusinessplan.com for more suggestions and tools on pricing.

Put your money where your mouth is by writing down your specific financial goal, as artist and author Violette Clark did.

Now that you've played with the numbers, summarize them in your Managing the Moola plan. You can do this by simply adding a few statements that answer the following questions:

- What are your sales goals?
- What are the different ways you will make money?
- How much do you want to make in profit?
- What are your expenses? What investments will you make in order to run, and grow, your business?

For example, your Managing the Moola plan might follow this format:

In _____ [year], I will make $_____ from my sales. [If you have multiple moola-making methods, you can break each one out by dollar amount or percentage. For example, a photographer might divide her income into the following categories: weddings, 50 percent of income; portraits, 20 percent; fine art, 20 percent; and photography workshops, 10 percent.]

I will sell _____ [amount]of _____ [pieces/items] at this price: _____. (Or: I will have _____ [number of] clients at this price: _____.)

The main areas I will spend money on are _____, _____, _____ [supplies, marketing, etc.], _____, and for these expenses I have allocated $_____, _____, _____.

Complete the following statements on index cards to put in your Right-Brain Business Plan:

In _____ [year], I will make $_____ from my sales [income].

I will pay myself $_____ [your salary].

> **TIP**
>
> In this chapter we've covered basic financial elements common to most businesses. Once you feel comfortable with this level, start to educate yourself more about the specific business models used in your industry. Perhaps talk to a mentor about how he or she structures pricing. That level of detail will be helpful if you need a loan or decide to seek investors.

I will sell/work with _____ [number of art pieces, of commissions, clients, packages, workshops, etc.] for this price: _____. [You might have multiple lines for this section if you have different moola-making methods.]

The main areas I will spend money on are _____, _____, and _____. I have allocated the following amounts of money to these expenses: _____, _____, _____.

My profit will be $_____ [total income minus expenses].

Suggested Actions to Take Now

- If you haven't already, create a separate business checking account and get a separate business credit card. Teasing apart your business expenses from your personal expenses will help you better track how you spend money.
- Collect your receipts and organize them in the same categories that you created from your pink sticky notes. This will give you information to start entering into a bookkeeping system.
- Start using a standard bookkeeping system. QuickBooks is one of the most popular and is widely used by bookkeepers and accountants. Once you input your data, computerized bookkeeping systems take care of calculations, and they have common reports — like the profit and loss statement, cash flow statement, and balance sheet — built in. An accountant or bookkeeper can help you set up your system.

The Payoff: What's This All For, Anyway?

You've put in such great work while figuring out the numbers, and you may be wondering what it's all for. The good news is that there's a payoff for your efforts. Having a sense of your financial picture empowers you to make informed decisions about your business: you can better predict how much money will be in your checking account and when, and you can feel the pride of seeing your earnings grow. By keeping tabs on your tab, you can see what's working and what's not, and you can make changes, such as in the amount you charge or what you spend money on.

To make sense of the numbers, look for any trends. Are the numbers going in the direction you want them to go? Ask yourself the tough questions, as in the following examples:

- Look at your bottom line. Are you hitting your financial goals? Are you making enough money?
- What would make a big difference in your profits?
- Are certain months really tight for you because of the natural cycle of your business? Can you make adjustments and spread your expenses across other months to improve your cash flow?
- When you look at your expenses, what big numbers stand out? Are there ways to reduce spending — for example, could you sublet your office or studio space one or two days a week, cancel memberships that you're not using, or buy supplies in bulk?
- Are there other things you could spend money on that would actually increase profit? For example, do you need to hire an assistant so you can focus more on moola-making activities?
- Where can you make more money? What other moola-making methods can you try? Where can you increase your prices?

Review your responses, and make any adjustments needed to your plan.

- Reframe your limiting beliefs about money and turn them into positive affirmations.
- Make your Moola Map.
- Plug your Moola Map numbers into the Rid the Red, Grow the Green template.
- Sum it all up in your Managing the Moola plan.

LEFT-BRAIN CHECKLIST

Before moving on to the next chapter, review the checklist below. Your left brain will thank you!

- ❏ I have identified how much moola I want to bring in, both in income and in profit.
- ❏ I have chosen my moola-making methods.
- ❏ I have determined my pricing.
- ❏ I have estimated my expenses.
- ❏ I have filled out my Rid the Red, Grow the Green spreadsheet and have a sense of how much money I will bring in this year.

BROWNIE POINTS

- ❏ I have a separate business checking account.
- ❏ I have a separate business credit card account.
- ❏ I have set up a bookkeeping system, or I have contacted a bookkeeper or accountant to help me.
- ❏ I have asked myself the tough questions about my financial picture.

6 Corralling Your Creative Cohorts

Build a Creative Playground of Business Support So You Don't Have to Go It Alone

As a creative, independent spirit, you may be used to doing things solo. No one else can do it quite like you can, right? Doing what you love should be the core of your business, and I have no doubt that you're the perfect person to do what you're passionate about. However, that doesn't mean you have to know every aspect of your business or do everything on your own. If you're bearing most of the burden, I bet you often feel isolated and burned-out. When you enlist support, you can focus on your interests and natural gifts, maintain better balance, and have more fun.

You're not alone on your entrepreneurial journey. If you haven't already, approach trusted friends, family members, and colleagues and let them know about your business vision and how they can help. Brainstorm with them to help flesh out your goals. Seek mentors, teachers, and connectors. Perhaps the perfect person to help you is someone from work, or an old classmate, your neighbor down the hall, your hairstylist, your doctor, or your mail carrier...you never know who they might know.

This chapter will help you get clear on what type of support you need for the different aspects of your business. Support comes in many forms: it may be pro bono or paid; it may come from friends or free-lancers; and it may take the form of advice, brainstorming, or encour-agement, or the form of someone holding you accountable when you promise to accomplish something, playing devil's advocate, or simply listening. Perhaps you need expert guidance on how to set up a blog or QuickBooks. Or you may just need a group of friends to give you feed-back on a new workshop you're creating. Who in your life is perfectly suited for that? Who do you need to seek out? Whatever form of help you need, there's bound to be a way to drum up support.

RIGHT-BRAIN REFLECTION

Take a moment to reflect on where you could use some extra hands in your work and life. If you could get all the help in the world, what type of assistance would you ask for?

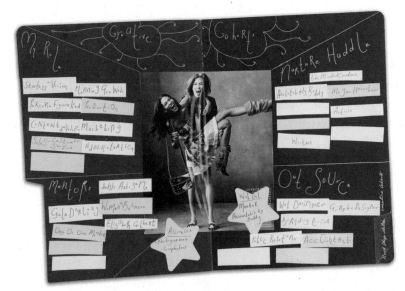

As Tanya Demello of My Little Life mapped out her creative cohorts, she realized that who she wanted most to help her grow her business was a mentor and an accountability buddy.

Write up a helping-hands wish list of everything in your business you need help with. Consider other areas in your life where you could use support, too. For example, I love that I can actually get work done while someone else is cleaning my house! Keep this list handy; you'll come back to it later.

Who's Who in Your Business

The following questions and exercises will help you identify who is, or needs to be, involved in your business. Your playground of creative cohorts can include a mix of full-time or part-time employees, freelancers for specific projects, an inner circle of advisors who provide guidance and expertise, strategic partners, wise mentors, and nurturing peers who provide feedback and support. If you're mostly right-brained, which left-brainers can help round you out? In which areas of your business are you less experienced? In which could you benefit from having an expert?

Your work in this chapter sets the stage for the section that would be titled "Management Team and Personnel" in a more traditional business plan.

Head Honcho Number One: Defining Your Role

Since you're the head honcho of your creative enterprise, let's start with information about you and the role you play. After all, your business is an extension of you. Then you can describe the rest of your creative cadre.

What do you bring to the table? How are you the perfect person to run the show?

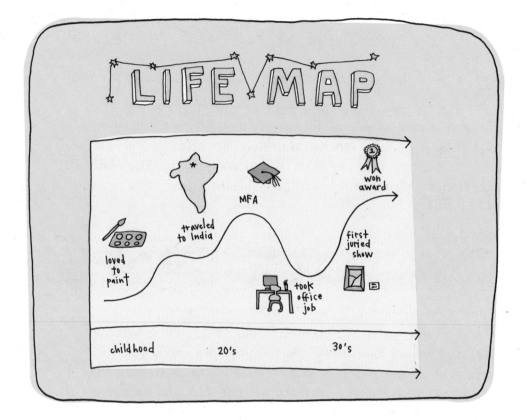

Create a life map illustrating the significant personal and professional milestones that make you the most qualified person to head up your business. Draw a horizontal line and mark time periods on it. Next, along the time line, plot out major milestones and achievements that relate to your leadership of your business. What were some key learning moments in your life? What have you done that is impressive? This is your opportunity to brag about yourself, so please don't be modest. If you have trouble thinking of things to include, have a friend or family member remind you of all your wonderful talents and accomplishments.

Include things about yourself such as the following:

- Education and training
- Qualifications
- Work experience
- Passions, interests, and relevant hobbies
- Accomplishments and awards
- Personal triumphs that demonstrate your character

You can translate your visual life map into a short written biography to include in your final plan, if needed. If you're talking with investors, this is your opportunity to explain why they should give you money.

Next, think about what role you see yourself playing in the company. I've listed a smorgasbord of the typical functions and tasks that go into running a business. Some may not apply to your line of work. Use a colored pen to circle the ones that you want responsibility for, that you enjoy, and that you're good at. Using another color, circle the remaining roles that need to be filled in your business, but that you may not have the skills or time for or interest in. The second set of circled roles will help you make decisions in the following sections about hiring a team and using outside services.

Typical functions or roles in a small business:

- Strategy and vision
- Planning to grow your business and make the most of potential opportunities
- Research and development for new products and services
- Production (for example, making the jewelry, doing the art, processing photos, etc.)
- Content development (for example, for service providers this could include writing articles or courses, or developing and packaging your services)
- Providing services to customers (for a service-based business)
- Marketing to reach more people
- Sales to increase money coming in
- Operations to keep your business systems and processes running smoothly

- Administrative tasks such as paperwork, scheduling, and other tactical work
- Finances, including the financial big picture, projections, and planning
- Billing and collecting payment
- Bookkeeping, including entering financial transactions — such as sales, payments to vendors, and refunds — in your financial records, as well as reconciling checking and credit card accounts
- Managing people by providing guidance, direction, and feedback to your employees
- Staffing your company, including hiring and firing workers
- Training and educating your team on how work gets done in your business

Use the items you circled to write a paragraph describing your role.

In Good Company: Hiring a Team

Maybe you own a boutique and you need to hire a few sales associates, or you're a graphic designer looking to expand your studio. If you're hiring employees, you'll need to consider some important topics, like who does what and how you'll structure your team. Look at the second set of roles you circled, plus your helping-hands wish list from earlier in the chapter, and see what items you want to hire employees to do. There are also some key questions to consider in the planning process:

- Will your employees be full-time or part-time?
- What are your employees' roles and responsibilities? Who is best suited to do what?
- What will the reporting structure look like? Will your employees report directly to you, or will there be other supervisors or managers in place? Sketch out a basic organizational chart so that you have a visual snapshot of the company.
- How will you compensate your employees — with an hourly rate or a salary? Will you need to set up a payroll system?
- Will your employees receive benefits? If so, what kind? How much will that cost your company?

- What type of training or development might your employees need? Will they require courses to gain certain skills or credentials, the costs of which you must cover? How much will that amount to?

When you're heading up a team, your leadership and management is crucial to the success of the business. Here are a few questions to reflect on: What's your leadership style? What are your strengths as a leader? What can your employees count on you for? What do you want to communicate to your team? (Remember that your Right-Brain Business Plan can help convey your company vision to your employees.)

Even if you don't have employees right now, how might your business expand in the future? Who might you need to hire to help your business grow? For example, perhaps you plan to bring on an apprentice in one year's time to help you assemble your jewelry designs. Or perhaps you want to hire an administrative assistant within three years to help you with paperwork and scheduling, plus a sales representative to take care of landing new accounts.

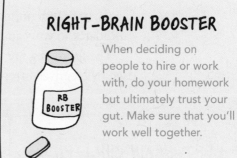

RIGHT-BRAIN BOOSTER

When deciding on people to hire or work with, do your homework but ultimately trust your gut. Make sure that you'll work well together.

At Your Service: Using Outside Services and Temporary Help

If you aren't hiring employees right now, but you know you need help with certain tasks or require specific expertise, consider enlisting outside services such as independent contractors, freelancers, consultants, or temporary help.

I cannot tell you how many tears I've shed over QuickBooks. When I first started out, and my business wasn't as complicated as it is now, I had the bookkeeping under control. After a while, though, I ended up with a big, ugly mess that sucked up way too much of my time. Eventually, I learned from that mistake and invested in a bookkeeper. Instead of pulling my hair out over an account that refuses to reconcile, I can now focus my time on building my business.

What drives you crazy in your business? What tasks require expertise that you don't really have? Where will delegating free you up to focus on doing what you love? Again, review the second set of circles you made on the list of business functions, along with your helping-hands wish list. Which tasks might you outsource? You might want to off-load some of the left-brain tasks that you loathe. Or perhaps there are a few right-brain activities that could use an extra helping of creative genius power.

Not sure how to start? Ask your friends, family, and colleagues for referrals, or search online. Take the time to talk with at least two or three candidates so you can make an informed decision.

The following are typical individuals who provide outside services used by creative entrepreneurs:

LEFT-BRAIN CHILL PILL

If you're fretting over how you can afford to hire all the creative cohorts you need, consider bartering. Exchange products or services with someone else who can benefit from what you have to offer. Think about which services would be of value to you. And what is your time worth? Make sure that it's a fair trade, that both parties are clear on the terms, and that you put the agreement in writing.

- An attorney to advise you on legal matters, such as choosing your business structure, protecting your intellectual property, and drawing up contracts
- A certified public accountant to prepare your taxes and give you the scoop on all things IRS-related
- A bookkeeper to create invoices, enter transactions into your financial system, reconcile your bank accounts, and manage your books
- An administrative assistant or virtual assistant to take care of the logistics, such as sending out your mailings, updating your blog, managing your distribution list, scheduling meetings, or handling paperwork (virtual assistants work from their home offices and use their own resources, so they are not considered employees)
- A branding consultant to help you develop a consistent, recognizable image and message for your business
- A marketing consultant to help you promote your business

- A publicist or PR agent to write press releases and help you get featured in magazines and newspapers, on radio and television
- A graphic designer to help you with all your visual needs, like designing a logo, a brochure, a website, a business card, product packaging, swag, and other material
- A copywriter to help you write text for your website, newsletter, blog, or brochure
- A proofreader or editor to polish your professional copy
- A web developer to help you set up a website or blog
- A tech guru (or at least someone who can help you when your computer has a virus or your printer won't work!)
- A business consultant or coach to help you clarify your business goals and hold you accountable for taking action
- A photographer to take your headshot or pictures of your products
- A sales rep to help sell your products to retailers
- An agent to help connect you with places that will license your artwork or publish your book
- An intern or temp to help you with administrative tasks or for a specific project

Who else might enhance your business?

> **TIP**
>
> When you're working with contractors, outside service providers, or temps, be very clear about what you're hiring them for and what your working agreements are. For example, what are the deliverables and due dates? Who owns the intellectual property? How will you work best together?
>
> - What type of outside contractors are you already working with?
> - What are their responsibilities and roles?
> - Who else might you need to hire, and when?
> - How much can you afford to spend on outside services?

A Match Made in Heaven: Forming Strategic Alliances

Imagine what you could do if you joined forces with the perfect partner to create a new product, or to offer a specific service, that neither of you could create, or offer, alone. Strategic alliances are great examples of instances in which two heads are better than one. Consider partnering with complementary entrepreneurs on projects, or aligning yourself with other organizations, to build your experience and exposure. In a strategic alliance, you team up to do a specific piece of work that mutually benefits both parties, but you remain separate companies.

For example, during the first couple of years on my own, I was a contract coach and leader for a few organizations. Associating myself with well-established, recognizable companies helped me gain more visibility and develop new skills, and at the same time I was helping the companies build their business.

Other examples of strategic alliances might look like these:

- An expressive art therapist, massage therapist, and Reiki healer share an office space, where they meet their individual clients. Each is a solopreneur, but by sharing overhead expenses such as rent and utilities they alleviate costs. Also, because their ideal-client bases overlap, they help each other market their services whenever any client comes to the space.
- A branding consultant and copywriter team up to codevelop and colead a teleseminar on how to develop effective content for a blog.
- A makeup artist and photographer host a headshot-taking event.
- A coach becomes an affiliate or licensee of a well-known coaching program, making content development and marketing much easier.

Questions to consider:

- What strategic alliances might complement your business?
- Who would be the ideal people for you to collaborate with? Even if you don't know exactly who these people would be, what qualities or attributes would make someone an ideal partner?
- How would you split responsibilities with your strategic partner?
- How would you divide expenses and profits?

Your Inner Circle: Assembling a Board of Advisors

Advisory board is one of those left-brain, corporate-sounding terms that may scare off a fun-loving, creative entrepreneur such as yourself. Different from the board of directors that is a legal requirement for a corporation or a nonprofit, an advisory board consists of volunteers who contribute their time, experienced insights, and expertise to help you grow your business. Think of your advisors as the important folks in your inner circle to go to for guidance, support, and feedback. Perhaps you invite into your inner circle of advisors a few friends who are brilliant marketers or social networkers, or a former colleague who has a background in finance, or fellow entrepreneurs in complementary fields whose opinions you trust. What areas of your business do you feel less knowledgeable about or lack experience in? Do you know some left-brain thinkers who can complement your right-brain sensibilities?

SUCCESS STORY

Julie Benjamin dreamed of one day opening Little Lane Studios, where children could take art classes, participate in collaborative creative projects, and learn about community service. Just as she would eventually teach her students to work together to accomplish a goal, she too needed to collaborate with others to make her vision real. At first, opening the studio seemed like a daunting task, full of unknowns. Things shifted for Julie when she reached out to her friends, colleagues, and supporters and invited them to a brainstorming session. In effect, she assembled her inner circle of advisors.

She included fellow teachers, people with a business background, her graphic designer, her business collaborator, friends, and family. She developed an agenda so she was clear about what she wanted to get out of the meeting. She also used her Big-Vision Collage to communicate her dream of not just the beautiful physical space but also the positive impact her studio would have on the children and the community. Her Right-Brain Business Plan helped rally her inner circle around her big vision. Receiving concrete feedback and visible support empowered Julie to take the next step in getting the studio off the ground. In return for their help, Julie offered her inner circle use of the studio space for their own creative endeavors.

Who will become your inner circle of advisors, or what type of people would you like to have? What will their roles and responsibilities be? Even if you don't have specific people in mind right now, write a description of the types of expertise you're seeking. By being clear on what types of contacts you're looking for, you will find it easier to identify those people as you do your research and networking.

It's up to you whether you formally assemble your inner circle of advisors or simply have an informal list of people to call on individually when you need expert guidance. If you want to officially gather your group, you can meet with your inner circle of advisors on a regular basis or when you need to make key decisions. The important thing is to be clear about what you're asking them to commit to in terms of time and resources. Also consider what's in it for them, especially since they'll most likely be volunteering their time. Maybe they'll value networking with other professionals in the circle. Or they'll do just about anything for one of your famous homemade red velvet cupcakes. Find ways to make the experience worth their while, too.

Surrounding yourself with good people bolsters your business in many ways. You round out areas that you may not have knowledge or expertise in, you gain valuable perspectives from trusted people, and you demonstrate to potential investors and customers that you have talented, experienced people behind you.

Additional Ideas for Getting Support

Here are several other structures and resources that can help you get the support you need:

Find an accountability buddy. If you're looking for an easy, no-cost way to get some help and to help someone else, partner with an accountability buddy. Choose a trusted colleague in the same, or a complementary, field and meet with him or her regularly, either in person, on the phone, or via email to report on progress, talk through issues, and celebrate successes. A typical meeting might last an hour, with each buddy having thirty minutes to focus on his or her issues. If you have someone in mind, reach out today. You never know what might happen. You can plan to meet with your buddy every week for the next three months, or meet once a month for a whole year. Just make sure that you're both clear about expectations and the time commitment.

Create a "nurture huddle." Creative blogger and collage artist Melba McMullin coined the term *nurture huddle* to describe a safe, collaborative gathering of peers who mutually encourage and inspire each other. A creative alternative to a traditional mastermind or accountability group, a nurture huddle is like cozying up with a nice cuppa tea and some wonderful friends as you dream about and grow your businesses. Surround yourself with positive people who will help you focus on what's working, and who will have constructive ideas for areas that aren't. Your huddlers will provide fresh perspectives, help you

further your business vision, hold you accountable for your commitments, believe in you even when you're doubting yourself, and celebrate your successes. Your huddlers will also give you a gentle, yet swift, kick in the pants when needed, to help you transform your vision into action. I entered into my nurture huddle with the goal of writing a book, and thanks to our biweekly calls, my huddlers helped me bring forth what you now hold in your hands.

The ideal group size is four to seven huddlers, so that each has ample time to share and the group feels intimate. Meet with your huddlers weekly or every other week, either in person or over the phone (see the Resources section at the back of this book for information on conference call lines), and have each huddler take a turn facilitating a ninety-minute session. Use email, a blog, or a private online community to stay connected between meetings.

TIP

The difference between a nurture huddle and your inner circle of advisors is that a nurture huddle is a forum in which all members of the group support each other. The group focuses on each member's business or project in turn. Your inner circle of advisors is structured so that the members all focus their creative energy and support solely on your business.

Hire a coach. When you want one-on-one professional support for achieving your goals, consider hiring a business or life coach. There are many different types of coaches out there. Some focus on a client's whole life; others work exclusively with entrepreneurs. Try several sample sessions to find the best fit for you. I've worked with several coaches over the years. They've been invaluable in helping me transition from corporate life to entrepreneurship, develop my products, work on this book, and so much more.

Seek out a mentor. Mentors will show you the ropes. They tend to have more experience than you in a particular area and can offer wisdom and insights. Mentors are all around you. I actually met one through Twitter. I searched on the keywords *expressive arts* and stumbled upon Chris Zydel, a creativity coach and expressive arts leader, only to discover serendipitously that her painting studio is ten minutes from my house. Be on the lookout for potential mentors. Take a class and see if you click with the teacher. Ask an old colleague out to lunch. Before you meet with your mentor, develop a list of your burning questions to guide your conversation. Be mindful of how you use her time, and also see how you can help her. See if you can design an ongoing relationship with her so she can support you throughout your journey, and always show your appreciation for her generosity.

Conduct a focus group. Perhaps you need targeted feedback for a specific project. Instead of pulling things out of thin air, gather members of your target audience together (or even just some friends, if you want something more casual) to test your ideas and offer suggestions. Be clear about what type of information you're seeking. Create an agenda and list of questions ahead of time to keep the group on track. Consider having someone else facilitate and take notes on the session so you can concentrate on what is being shared.

Cultivating New Connections

As you've gone through the exercises in this chapter, you may not have been able to identify specific people to assist you in all the areas you need help in. That's okay. It just means you get to meet some new people. Cultivating new connections expands your horizons, creates unexpected opportunities, and can surprise you with new-found colleagues, allies, and friends. Plus, you'll be surprised to know that many people love hearing inspiring stories about the creative process and about go-getters such as yourself who are living their dreams, so don't shy away from sharing your entrepreneurial journey. In chapter 4, you practiced having a meaningful dialogue about your work. Continue honing that message as you communicate to new people what you do.

Here are some really simple ways to connect:

- Say hello to someone in the elevator or on the bus.
- Strike up a conversation with the cashier at the grocery store or with someone waiting in line with you.
- Comment on a blog that inspires you.
- Go to a networking event or class and get to know at least one new person (maybe she's that cool gal next to you at yoga tonight).

SUCCESS STORY

One of my clients was building her coaching practice, so I challenged her to talk about her business to random people she interacted with throughout the day. In just a few days, she had enrolled a local bank teller and a customer-service phone representative for sample sessions, and one of them became a client of hers. She was surprised at how easy it was to share her vision with people she didn't even know, how open they were to engaging with her, and how she was able to make a positive impact in a short amount of time.

- Introduce one of your friends to someone you think she should know, and spread the good connection karma.
- Set up a coffee date with someone at work you've wanted to get to know better.
- Make it a goal to talk to five new people each day for the next week.

Mapping Out the Company You Keep

TRACEY ASAI
D E S I G N S

The Wedding Party

Bride
Tracey Asai
Designer/Owner

Groom
William Asai
Inner Circle Advisor

Maid of Honor
J. Simon
Public relations

Best Man
R. Tenez
Die maker/clicking contractor

Bridesmaids
Seamstress

Ushers
C.J.
Online wedding
marketing consultant

Carpenter/craftsman

R.G.
Trim/sewing contractor

M.L.
Fabric-fusing contractor

Assistant
Intern from F.I.T.

Computer technician
PC Tune-Up Pros

Host and technical support
Citymax.com

Tracey Asai of Tracey Asai Designs creates wedding flip-flops, so it's no wonder that her Creative Cohorts Visual Map uses the format of a wedding party chart. What metaphor works for your business?

In this chapter, you've started to identify all the people you'll tap to help you make your business successful. Now let's map out the company that you keep. Use the Creative Cohorts play sheet on page 140 to list each creative cohort, as in the example shown, or you can jump straight to creating the visual map. List the names of your cohorts and include their areas of expertise or the roles you want them to play on your team. Also, keep in mind that, although you may not know the name of a particular individual yet, you know what type of person you need, so write that down.

It's not about the size of your team. It's about the quality of your players. It's okay if only a few people make up your core creative cohorts. You might add more people as you learn more about where your business is headed. You might call on different people at different times to help out with a specific challenge or task. See page 139 for an example of how you can identify your creative cohorts.

Example of Creative Cohort List
for Yoga Instructor/Workshop Leader

NAME	AREA OF EXPERTISE	ROLE	SPECIFIC REQUESTS TO MAKE OF COHORTS, OR ACTIONS TO TAKE (INCLUDING TIMING)
Mary	Marketing, promotions, and social media	Inner circle of advisors	Join my inner circle of advisors to provide expert guidance on marketing. Meet for an hour every quarter.
Elle	Finance (she's a VP of finance for a corporation)	Inner circle of advisors	Join my inner circle of advisors to provide expert guidance on business finances. Meet for an hour every quarter.
Jenna	Well networked in the start-up community	Inner circle of advisors	Join my inner circle of advisors to provide expert guidance on launching a business. Meet for an hour every quarter. Help me connect with other entrepreneurs.
Susan	Established yoga studio owner who leads international retreats	Mentor	I will schedule a 60-minute phone call with Susan by next Friday to ask her what it was like to open up a studio.
Kelly	Graphic design	Outside services — freelance designer	Ask Kelly for a quote on a new logo by September 30.
Mike	QuickBooks	Outside services — bookkeeper	Send my receipts and bank statements to Mike by the 20th of each month so he can reconcile my accounts.
Chris	Writing	Outside services — copywriter	Ask Chris to write copy for my new website by September 30.
TBD	Commercial real estate and lease agreements	Outside services — commercial real estate agent	When I'm ready to start looking for a studio space, I will contact a commercial real estate agent to help me find the perfect location.
TBD	Business insurance	Insurance representative	Sign up for business liability insurance.
Lesli Debra Emily Sarah	Emotional support and accountability	Nurture huddle	Meet in a facilitated conference call for 90 minutes every other week for the next year. Help hold each other accountable for our business goals.

Even if you have a slew of people helping you, they may not always be in plain sight. Perhaps you work from your home office and your assistant, bookkeeper, and sales agent all live in different states. Maybe your inner circle of advisors meets face-to-face only once a quarter, and your nurture huddle connects virtually via the phone. Keep your team close at hand by making a visual map of your creative cohorts. This image will give you a sense of how your team supports the big picture, and it will also remind you that you are not alone.

A Creative Cohorts play sheet is provided for you to use as inspiration, but feel free to make your Creative Cohorts Visual Map in any format that inspires you. Other structures that you might use: a creative cohorts tree, with branches for each grouping of support; or a body diagram, with each body part representing a function in your company (for example, the eyes can be people who help you envision your business goals, the hands can be people who help you by doing tasks, and the heart can be your nurture huddle). Your visual map is yet another opportunity for you to use your creative license.

What you'll need:

- A large sheet of paper (poster size or from a flip chart)
- Markers
- Sticky notes (optional)
- Photos of team members (optional) or images clipped from magazines to represent the people you'd like on your team
- Tape or a glue stick

Instructions: Affix the large sheet of paper to a wall. Map out all the people who support you in your business. List their names and roles. If you have pictures, put a face to the name and personalize your map even further. You can also use sticky notes to write the names down so you can move them around or group them in categories. I've suggested some categories, but feel free to group your creative cohorts in whatever way makes most sense for you and your business.

- Employees
- Outside services, including freelancers, professional service providers, and temporary help
- Inner circle of advisors
- Nurture huddle for emotional support, encouragement, ideas, accountability, and brainstorming
- Mentors
- Virtual mentors, such as celebrities, famous fictional characters, spiritual guides, luminaries in your field, or other people you might not actually know but admire and want to learn

from; perhaps you want certain qualities or energy to inspire your business thinking

- Infrastructure support, such as operations, technology, administrative tasks, and bookkeeping
- Thought partners, such as people who can help you create products or relationships that become strategic alliances

What other types of groupings can you think of?

RIGHT-BRAIN REFLECTION

- Step back and look at your Creative Cohorts Visual Map. What do you notice?
- Where do you still have some gaps? What can you do to fill those gaps?
- If you were to give your team of creative cohorts a name, what might it be? Is there a metaphor, color, or phrase that represents the collective power?

Let's Play!

Next, invite your creative cohorts to join your playground. Let them know what you're up to in your business, and why you need their specific help. I've included a sample invitation, but feel free to craft your own. Get creative about how you send it. Maybe you'll use a party invitation that you get at a stationery store. Or perhaps you'll hand-stamp your own cards. Or maybe it will be a simple email that includes a picture of your Big-Vision Collage to inspire recipients and get them on board.

Dear _____,

I am embarking on an exciting entrepreneurial adventure, and I need your help. As you may know, I'm launching [or expanding] my business. [Include more details here and insert photos of your Right-Brain Business Plan.]

I know I can't do this alone. Plus, it's more fun with playmates. So, I've formed my own playground of creative cohorts. I want you to be a part of my professional community of supportive and trusted friends, colleagues, experts, mentors, and advisors who provide me with guidance and inspiration along my entrepreneurial journey.

You are . . . [Write down what you look to them for; for example: You are always so skilled at coming up with concrete action items. Or: You are an expert at marketing, or a great listener.] Would you be willing to . . . [Put your specific request here; for example: Would you be willing to be part of my inner circle of advisors, which meets quarterly for an hour to help me guide my business, or spend an hour with me over coffee so I can ask you about how you started your business]?

Please let me know. I appreciate your time and consideration.

I'd love to hear any questions you may have, and how I can support you in reaching your goals and dreams, too. Let's play together!

Sincerely,
[Your name goes here]

Suggested Actions to Take Now

In the next week, do the following:

- Talk about your business to ten people you already know, and enlist at least three of them to actively help you with specific requests. Perhaps they will simply volunteer to be the person you inform when you complete a goal, to help hold you accountable. Next, tell ten more people you're not acquainted with about your business, and ask at least two of them for specific support. For example, check out a website and then email or call the contact person there. Attend a meeting or networking event or tell a random person on the train about your business. The point is to get out there and stretch yourself.

- Join online social networks to see which people your friends and contacts know.
- Choose two or three things from the helping-hands wish list you made at the beginning of the chapter and identify at least one or two ways you can get support for each wish you selected. Brownie points: Reach out to someone today and ask for the help you need, based on your list.

You've done a great job of identifying the people whose help you need in order to make your entrepreneurial endeavors successful. Running a creative business can be challenging. And it can also be lots of fun when you invite others to play with you.

- Write your helping-hands wish list.
- Create a life map.
- Make a Creative Cohorts Visual Map or fill out the Creative Cohorts play sheet.

LEFT-BRAIN CHECKLIST

Before moving on to the next chapter, review the checklist below. Your left brain will thank you!

- ❏ I have clarified what my role is as head of my business.
- ❏ I have determined whether I need to hire employees, how many, and what their roles might be.
- ❏ I have identified where and when I might need to outsource work, and estimated how much that might cost.
- ❏ I have identified my inner circle of advisors (optional).
- ❏ I have identified my nurture huddle (optional).
- ❏ I have identified mentors (optional).
- ❏ I have identified potential strategic alliances (optional).
- ❏ I have sent my creative cohorts invitations to join my playground (optional).

7 Action Planning – Where the Rubber Meets the Road

Make Your Plan Real with Goals, Strategies, and Action Steps

 ow that you have a big vision for your business and you know where you want to head, you may be wondering, "Okay, what's next?" Well, in order to move forward, you need a plan of action. As a creative person, you may find that structure and planning are not your favorite things. Don't worry. In this chapter, you'll learn some simple tools and creative systems for getting into action.

Action makes your Right-Brain Business Plan real. Without action, your business plan is just a pretty piece to look at. Your collage will hang there collecting dust on the wall, your spreadsheet will never see the light of day, and you'll be wondering why you don't have more customers and why there isn't more money in your bank account.

Forget that scenario! You want to bring your plan to life and manifest your business vision soon. By doing the following exercises, you'll define the specific goals, strategies, and action steps needed to make your vision real. If your Right-Brain Business Plan is the visual map of where you want to go with your business, then the goals, strategies, and action steps are the landmarks, routes, and turn-by-turn directions to guide you to your desired destination.

Up until now, you've leveraged your right-brain brilliance in order to envision and explore. At this point in your business plan, however, your left brain gets to play a bigger role. Your logical left brain is your ally in articulating details, sequencing steps, and analyzing options — all critical skills in the area of action planning.

Moving through Fear

Is all this talk of action making you break into a cold sweat? This is indeed where the rubber meets the road, so it's natural for fears to surface. Fears are worth addressing here, because as you move your business

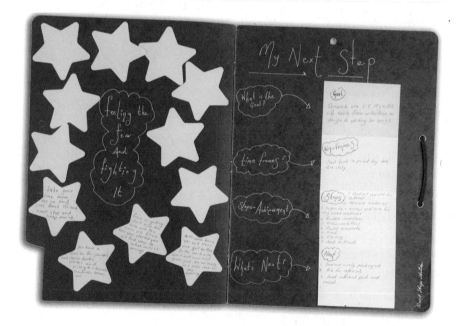

To move past her fears, Tanya Demello jotted down her doubts and worries. Then she covered up each fear with encouraging solutions written on star-shaped sticky notes to remind her of what she needs to do to take the next step.

boldly into the world — as I know you will — you'll undoubtedly encounter a few fears. Common limiting beliefs that prevent entrepreneurs from action planning include the following:

I'm not going to get it right. Let's face it, as an entrepreneur you take risks; they're inherent in your role. You don't have a crystal ball (or if you do, I'd love to borrow it!), so it's true, you aren't going to get it right 100 percent of the time. If you're a Type A, that's a hard pill to swallow. But rather than avoid action altogether, look at mishaps as learning opportunities. The more you learn, the more you and your business will grow.

I'm afraid I'll find out that my business isn't viable after all. So many people would rather stay in the dark about their business because they're worried that, by digging into the details and taking action, they'll discover they can't sustain themselves. What they may not realize is that the business plan is not that black and white. In fact, it's more like a blank canvas that you get to experiment on. If one part of the business is stuck, what variables can you adjust?

Action planning is too hard. I just wish someone else would do it for me. As we saw in the preceding chapter, about creative cohorts, you don't have to do everything on your own. It is important, though, for you as the business owner to be clear about what goals, strategies, and action steps will support your business vision. No one else can tell you the direction to point your company. Yes, you can ask for feedback and you can delegate tasks, but the vision of your company is yours, and the action planning is what makes that vision real. The good news is, with the steps outlined in this chapter, you'll discover that action planning is much easier than you may have thought. And, heaven forbid, you might even have fun with the right-brain approaches suggested at the end of the chapter.

If I put something down on paper and don't accomplish it, then I've failed — that's it, end of story. Oh, what a catch-22 this nasty belief creates! If you write it down, you might fail, but if you don't write it down, it may never happen. I've worked with many clients who hesitate writing down specific goals or sharing them with other people. They're afraid that if they proclaim, "I will land twenty new clients by the end of this month," and get only fifteen, then they'll have disappointed themselves and others. But if they don't write a specific target down, they'll always be shooting in the dark. They won't know if and when they've reached their goal, or if they need to make adjustments. By writing your goals down on paper, you're more likely to take action and make them happen, because to meet a specific, tangible goal, you'll have to come up with steps to reach it. And by the way, fifteen new clients is way better than no new clients, don't you think?

If I plan too much, I'll box myself in. For big-picture, creative thinkers, a plan can feel like the kiss of death. The action plan seems set in stone, stifling all innovation and freedom. But instead of feeling locked into your action plan, think of it as a fun playpen with flexible guardrails and plenty of colorful toys. You have the space to try new things and explore. Plus, you can always adjust the guardrails as needed. You can even tear them down and build new ones.

Taking action means this is real ... gulp! Yes, taking action says you mean business — whether you're opening your doors for the first time or you're launching a new product. While it can be scary, know that with each step forward you'll gain more momentum and confidence.

Goals, Strategies, and Action Steps

The following structure is a standard breakdown of goals, strategies, and action steps used by MBAs and Fortune 500 companies alike — but with a right-brain twist, of course. This method will help you articulate what you want to achieve and how you're going to achieve it.

Goals: The "What"

We start off by defining goals. At the highest level, goals are what you want to achieve. Your goals support your overall business vision and plan. You will probably have goals that address the different parts of your Right-Brain Business Plan, such as Getting the Word Out goals, Managing the Moola goals, or other big-vision goals.

Make sure that each goal meets all of the SMART guidelines (that it's specific, measurable, achievable, resonant, and time-bound). If it meets these five guidelines, you'll know the goal is clear.

Specific. The more specific details, the better. With specifics, you'll know if you reached your target or not. Instead of "Get more clients," a specific goal for a photographer might look like this: "In the next three months, I will book 6 more destination weddings and 4 more local weddings for next year, and I will shoot 8 baby portrait sessions." Instead of "I will increase my media exposure," a more specific goal would be: "My company and/or products will have been featured in 20 or more media outlets (including print, TV, radio, and Web) by December 31, 2011."

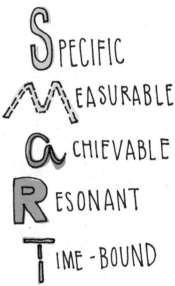

Measurable. What quantifiable metrics, such as number, frequency, duration, or percentage, can you use to keep track of your goal and measure your results? For example, you might settle on the following: "In the first quarter of this year, I will sell 100 sterling silver bracelets, 50 gold bracelets, and 20 gemstone bracelets." Sometimes the "measurable" criteria and "specific" criteria overlap, and that's okay.

Achievable. Taking into account your current resources (including time, money, and support), is your goal attainable? Your goals should stretch you, but they should not frustrate you because they are out of reach.

Consider questions such as the following:

- Do I have enough time to reach this goal? If not, what help or assistance might I need to make this goal achievable within the given time frame?
- Do I have the skills or capabilities necessary to make this happen? If not, do I have the time and money to get the

training this goal requires? Do I have the money to hire someone who has these skills?

- ◆ What resources do I need to tap into? Oftentimes we need help from other people or require additional information or skills, so don't overlook the importance of support.

Resonant. Here's where we bring in the right-brain twist. The Coaches Training Institute, the coaching industry leader, substitutes "R for reso-

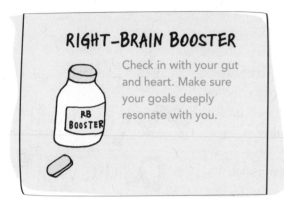

RIGHT-BRAIN BOOSTER

Check in with your gut and heart. Make sure your goals deeply resonate with you.

nant" for the standard "R for relevant." The more aligned the goal is with your values and vision, the more likely you will dedicate the time and energy necessary to achieve the goal. If it feels like a burdensome "have-to," the goal probably isn't going to be met. Having a joyful emotional connection to the goal will spur you to take action because you want to. Do a gut check. Is the goal meaningful to you? How much does this goal make your heart sing?

Time-bound. By what date will you accomplish this goal? Specifying a date gives you a target to shoot at. A deadline also makes it clear whether you achieved your goal or not, giving you room for realistic adjustments, if needed.

I'll use the following example of a SMART goal to walk you through the next two sections about breaking the goal down into strategies and action steps: "By December 31, 2011, I'll have $30,000 in my business bank account after I've paid all my expenses and taxes."

Strategies: The "How"

For each goal, you'll define a set of strategies. Strategies are your methods — how you are going to achieve your goals. You can (and should) have multiple strategies for each of your goals; that way you're not putting all your eggs in one basket. You might want to brainstorm five to ten possible strategies before narrowing the list down to two or three. In fact, you probably identified some potential strategies in the work you did in chapters 4 and 5. As you outline the goals, strategies, and action steps described in this chapter, you'll bring all those ideas into one place and prioritize them. Also, the creative systems for jump-starting your action planning discussed later in this chapter might help you to identify various strategies.

Let's look again at my sample SMART goal: "By December 31, 2011, I'll have $30,000 in my business bank account after I've paid all my expenses and taxes." To bring this goal and possible strategies to life, let's meet Robert. Robert is a visual artist who primarily paints large oil landscapes. His midrange pieces average two thousand dollars each, and his mural landscapes average seventy-five hundred dollars. In addition to exhibiting in galleries, he enjoys showing his work at art shows and has been quite successful at several shows in his home state of California. He would also like to earn about 20 percent of his income through licensing his work.

Based on this scenario, some strategies Robert might use to achieve his goal include the following:

- Strategy #1: Sell fifteen midrange paintings at five art shows in 2011.
  - At an average of two thousand dollars per painting, he will earn thirty thousand dollars, minus expenses.
  - He plans to sell three pieces at each show.
  - Based on his Managing the Moola plan, Robert knows that about 10 percent of the cost of a painting goes to raw materials, and that his show expenses average about one thousand dollars, which he spends on travel, promotional postcards, booth rental, application fees, and hiring a person to help him at his booth. So, he will spend about three thousand dollars on materials for the fifteen paintings, and a total of three

RIGHT-BRAIN BOOSTER

Get into the groove by taking a quick walk outside. Moving your body will help move your mind into action.

thousand on expenses for the three shows. That means he will have twenty-four thousand dollars left after expenses.

- Strategy #2: Hire a sales rep by April 30, 2011, and have the rep sell four large landscape murals at seventy-five hundred each for a total of thirty thousand dollars. After paying a 40 percent commission to the sales rep and taking into account the 10 percent cost of raw materials, Robert will earn fifteen thousand.
- Strategy #3: License work to three greeting card companies by the end of the third quarter. This will account for 20 percent or more of his income (that is, around ten thousand dollars).

Robert will be paying an estimated nineteen thousand dollars in taxes (close to 40 percent of his income). At the end of the year, he will have thirty thousand dollars left in his bank account. Based on these projected strategies, he can meet his goal.

LEFT-BRAIN CHILL PILL

Feeling action overload and not sure where to start? Prioritize your goals, and focus first on the ones that are most critical. And, at any given time, have at least one simple goal and one difficult goal. The simple one will give you confidence and keep you motivated, and the difficult one will keep you challenged and on your game.

Action Steps: The "To-Dos"

Action steps are the detailed, practical tasks you need to perform to achieve your goals. These can look like the familiar to-do list. By breaking the strategies down into discrete tasks, you'll be better able to plan for resources and timing. You'll be able to tackle your goals piece by piece, instead of feeling that you have to do everything all at once and getting overwhelmed.

Robert's SMART goal: "By December 31, 2011, I'll have $30,000 in my business bank account after I've paid all my expenses and taxes." And one strategy: "I'll sell fifteen midrange paintings at five art shows in 2011." Some possible action steps include:

- By January 1, 2011, identify five or six local art shows to participate in this year.

- Determine if shows are juried.
  - If juried, prepare an application and photos for each show (due dates vary according to the show deadlines).
- Develop postcards to promote the shows (twelve weeks before the show).
  - Find a designer to design the postcards (twelve weeks before the show).
  - Find a printer to print the postcards (eight weeks before the show).
  - Buy postage (four weeks before the show).
  - Create mailing labels from mailing list (four weeks before the show).
  - Send out postcards (three weeks before the show).

If your to-dos are not aligned to a specific goal, then you're just running around haphazardly, trying to check things off your list. That's just plain exhausting and ultimately won't get you where you want to go. SMART goals, strategies, and action steps will help you focus your time and energy. And they will support you in successfully implementing your Right-Brain Business Plan.

Custom rug designer Danielle David Grinnen of Deliante Designs wrote her goals and action steps on slips of paper that she tucked into decorative pockets on her vibrant visual plan.

Complete SMART Goal play sheets for your top three or four goals, including the supporting strategies and action steps. You'll need one play sheet for each goal. Stick to just those three or four goals right now to avoid becoming overwhelmed, but know that you can always add more goals later. Your goals can be anything that will support your business plan and your overall vision.

In the next week, tell at least five people about five actions you are committed to taking. Then do at least one of your action steps within the next week.

S.M.A.R.T. goal

S.M.A.R.T. goal (what you want to achieve):

STRATEGIES (how you'll achieve the goal)	ACTION STEPS (the to-do's)	SUPPORT/ RESOURCES needed	TARGET DATE	actual DATE completed
1.				
2.				
3.				

PLAY SHEET

If the structured SMART Goal play sheet confines your right-brain sensibilities, feel free to create your own visual that will help you track your progress. The important thing is that you're clear about what needs to happen to attain your goals, and that you have a way to measure results. Or, if you find yourself getting caught up in defining the goals "correctly" or putting them into the "right" hierarchy, just notice that your left brain is asserting itself and wants everything to make perfect, logical sense. That's fine, unless it's preventing you from getting anything down on paper. If you're blocked as you attempt to define goals, strategies, and action steps, here are four creative suggestions for jump-starting your action-planning ability. Use these tools individually or in combination to help you map out your actions.

Write a letter to yourself from the future. If you're not sure how to get started with your planning, whip out a pen and paper and write a letter to yourself from the future. Date it one year from now. Begin with "Dear Me . . . What an exciting year I've had . . ." Next, in as much detail as possible, describe what you accomplished in the past year. Were you on the *Today* show? Did you break six figures? What process did you go through to reach your goals? What did it take to get there? What were the challenges you faced, and how did you overcome them? What did the experience feel like? Allow yourself to be as creative and lavish as you want! Have fun imagining what's possible. This exercise is not about being realistic; it's about getting your creative juices flowing.

Once you're done writing, go back and review your letter. Circle any phrases or sections that sound like potential action steps that would support your goals. Even if what you wrote is more extravagant than your down-to-earth SMART goals, your future letter offers clues to action steps. While you may not get on the *Today* show (at least not yet!), if media exposure is part of your strategy, think about what steps you need to take to get on TV. You probably need a press release and a media kit. You may hire a publicist. Identify which TV shows you want to pitch. It's easier to work backward, by pretending it's already happened.

Build on what you know. As you identify the action steps that will support your goals and strategies, you may find that you're not sure what to do. When that happens, use something you're already familiar with to gain clarity about tackling an unfamiliar task. For example, how is baking brownies like building a blog? What's the first thing you do when you prepare to whip up some chocolaty treats? By walking through the steps of something you know, you'll discover your own creative resourcefulness, and new tasks will feel less daunting.

Example of Building on What You Know

HOW BAKING BROWNIES IS...	LIKE BUILDING A BLOG
Find the right recipe.	Find the right blog template.
Preheat the oven.	Choose the domain name.
Gather all the ingredients.	Brainstorm the different page elements.
Measure the ingredients.	Outline the content.
Mix the wet ingredients with the dry ingredients.	Lay out the content using the design template.
Lick the spoon.	Do a test post.
Pour batter into a pan.	Upload your first batch of content.
Bake for one hour; check for doneness by poking a toothpick in the center.	Launch your site and monitor stats and comments for the first two weeks; make adjustments as needed.

Make mind maps. Mind maps integrate both right-brain and left-brain thinking by capturing your stream of consciousness in a structured way. This method is perfect for brainstorming goals and organizing related ideas. Start with your goal or strategy in the middle of your diagram and then create branches of related ideas or action steps. You can group related

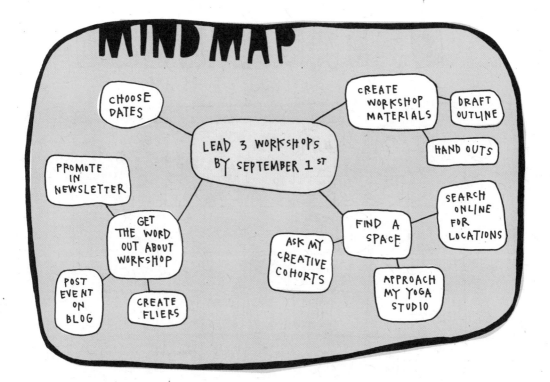

ideas together in circles and connect them to others with arrows or lines. Use colors, images, and words to help you visualize your plan. Add deadlines and resources to each action step bubble, and — voilà! — you have a mind-map action plan!

Play with the sticky-note project plan. If detailed project plans overwhelm you, try planning with sticky notes instead. Write each task on a sticky note as it comes to mind. Use different colors to categorize. Then begin arranging the notes on a large piece of paper pinned on a wall. You can draw rows on the paper to show weeks or months, and then start sequencing the notes on a time line. Sometimes it's helpful to work backward from the goal. So if launching your new product by the end of the year is your goal, what happens right before the launch? Keep working backward until you get to the first step. The cool thing about using sticky notes is that your plan isn't set in stone. You can easily move the notes around as you gain more clarity about what's next.

STICKY NOTE
PROJECT PLAN

TIP

As you review your actions, determine if there are any costs involved that were not accounted for in your Rid the Red, Grow the Green template. By getting clearer on the steps required to implement your plan, you likely have discovered that further investment is needed. Make sure you include these new costs in your Managing the Moola plan.

While you might be a right-brain entrepreneur, you can tap into your left-brain skills too in a fun, creative way. These suggestions are just some ways to structure your creative ideas to help you take action and move forward. Try one or two of them and see what shifts in your action-planning process.

Requests and Accountability

Your business vision doesn't exist in a vacuum. No doubt you're going to need people to help you with some of the tasks on your plan. Making clear, powerful requests and setting accountability are two skills that will help keep your business plan alive, especially as you engage others in your vision.

But as an independent, creative spirit, you may shy away from asking for help. You can do it better by yourself, right? Wouldn't it take more time to explain to someone how to do it than to just do it yourself? While it may seem easier to be the martyr, in the end your business will suffer and you'll burn yourself out. Having a business plan helps you to be strategic about how you allocate your time and resources.

Making Requests

So how do you ask for help? Are you the "read-my-mind" type of person? While you're in the car with a friend, do you mutter, almost under your breath, "It's sure getting cold in here, isn't it?" when what you really want to ask is: "Will you please roll up your window now?"

A complaint is usually a request in disguise. In your work, what do you find yourself complaining about? Are you frustrated with the bookkeeping? Do you wish your marketing-whiz brother-in-law would give you some pointers? These could be clues to what you might request help with.

Look over your action plan and identify where you indicated that you'd need support or resources. What would you like to ask for, and who would you like to ask? You might ask your inner circle of advisors, your friends, a contractor, or an intern. For example, you might send a message out to your friends, asking, "Will you review my new website copy and give me feedback on its tone and message by June 1?"

A specific request is: "Will you [do something] by [this date]?" The clearer you are about your request, the more likely you'll get the support or help you need. Plus, people will know exactly how they can help you.

Remember that it's acceptable for the other person to say no. Not everyone will have the capacity or time to jump on board and fulfill your request right now, or be interested in doing so, and that's perfectly fine. Don't make it all about you and what you're up to.

Here's a way to build the asking-for-help muscle. Over the next twenty-four hours, make at least twenty requests. You could ask for directions, ask someone to hold a door open for you, ask your neighbor for a cup of sugar (even if you don't need it), or ask your mom to babysit this weekend so you and your sweetie can go on a date.

Creating Accountability

It's one thing to say you're going to do something, and another thing to actually do it. Structuring your accountability will help ensure that you keep your word. Accountability includes specifying what you are going to do and by when (which you've probably already defined in the SMART Goal play sheet). Accountability also defines how you and/or others will know the task was completed.

Here are some ideas to keep you on track:

- If you need to get your finances in order, schedule a meeting with your bookkeeper and commit to having all your receipts and statements organized by then to hand off to her.
- If you need to brush up on your public speaking skills, ask a friend to go to Toastmasters with you every week for a month.
- Ask your accountability buddy to check in with you by email at the end of each day to see if you wrote for one hour.
- Set up a blog in which you start sharing your goals and posting your actions. By having to report on your progress to "the world," you're more likely to keep your word. Plus, you'll probably inspire others to get moving on their goals, too.
- Work with a coach to set up commitments and report back to him about your progress.

Accessing Your Action Plan

Because your action plan contains more of the day-to-day tasks, this is probably the piece of your Right-Brain Business Plan that you'll connect with most often. Make sure it's readily available. And remember that it's a living, breathing document you can update and refine. In chapter 9, you'll find some tips on how to keep your Right-Brain Business Plan alive, what to do when your plan isn't working, and how to make adjustments.

- Complete SMART Goal play sheets for your top three or four goals.
- Try one or two of the suggested creative planning tools.

LEFT-BRAIN CHECKLIST

Before moving on to the next chapter, review the checklist below. Your left brain will thank you!

❏ My goals are SMART, and they align with my overall vision and values.

❏ I have multiple strategies for my goals. I'm not keeping all my eggs in one basket.

❏ I have clear action steps that support my goals and strategies.

❏ Based on my goals, strategies, and action steps, I have made adjustments as needed to my Getting the Word Out plan.

❏ Based on my goals, strategies, and action steps, I have made adjustments as needed to my Managing the Moola plan.

❏ I have made adjustments as needed to my Creative Cohorts Visual Map.

Weaving It All Together

Put the Finishing Touches on Your Right-Brain Business Plan

Throughout this creative planning process, you've delved into specific sections of your business plan. You've looked at your big vision, your business landscape, your perfect customers, your numbers, your goals, and your actions. Whew, how's that for getting a handle on this crazy thing called a business plan? Yay, you! Now you get to integrate all the different parts in a way that inspires you. It's as if you've gathered swatches of exquisite fabric and you're ready to sew them into a magnificent patchwork quilt. With your finished piece, you'll be able to step back and see how it all fits together and where your plan is taking you.

This chapter will help you put the finishing touches on your plan, including crafting any outstanding sections and adding any crowning embellishments. We'll make sure there aren't any pieces missing. Plus, we'll explore how to tailor your visual plan to suit the suits, if a loan or investor backing is what's needed next in your business.

Wedding flip-flop and accessory designer Tracey Asai bound several pocket folders together to create two large accordion books (one shown here). The front and back covers of the two books display her Perfect Customer Portraits, Business Self-Portrait, and Big-Vision Collage. The inside pockets hold detailed information about her finances, customers, marketing, and more.

EXERCISE

Integrating Your Plan in an Inspiring and Visual Way

As you've gone through the creative exercises in this book, you may have already started to integrate the different pieces of your plan in your own unique, visual way. That's fantastic. Continue doing what works for you. Otherwise, to get the ball rolling, I'll share some ideas about how you can bring the different pieces together. The best source of inspiration, however, is your own creative license, so trust that. Always.

Gather all the parts of your Right-Brain Business Plan that you've created so far. This could include your Big-Vision Collage, your completed play sheets, notes, images, your Perfect Customer Portraits, and any of the other artwork. Lay them out on a table or the floor so you can see them all together.

If, at the beginning of the book, you didn't decide what medium(s) you would use in order to assemble your visual plan, give yourself permission to get inspired right now.

a pocket holding cards that describe products & services or your marketing tactics

Either flip back to chapter 1 to see some suggested formats, look at the examples in this chapter and throughout the book, or simply follow your muse. When you see all your material spread out in front of you, what calls out to you?

SUCCESS STORY

Artist Earleen Stanwaity of Ethereal Enterprises, LLC, creates intuitive carvings and artwork for ceremonies, altars, and rituals. She followed her intuition when she designed the fun format for her Right-Brain Business Plan. The collaged pages of her visual plan are tucked into clear plastic covers that she clipped to a length of embroidery thread so that the pages hang like clothes on a clothesline. The plastic covers make it easy for her to see the contents, and they help to keep her sticky notes and paper-clipped note cards in place. Since making her plan, she has gained more clarity about her market, has moved her website, and is working on her marketing strategies. She has hung her Right-Brain Business Plan in her studio to remind her of her vision and her goals, and loves that it's a work in progress.

Artist Earleen Stanwaity of Ethereal Enterprises used large square pieces of colored cardstock to craft her Right-Brain Business Plan, with each page focusing on a separate piece of her plan.

Create a Pullout calendar for timelines & milestones

If you are drawn to the idea of consolidating everything into a compact, portable format, try an art journal or an accordion book. You can paste your Big-Vision Collage into the journal or accordion book, along with your Perfect Customer Portraits, your Business Self-Portrait, your Getting the Word Out and Managing the Moola goals, your Creative Cohorts Visual Map, and your action plan. You can fold up your play sheets and tuck them into envelopes that you glue to the pages.

SUCCESS STORY

Pascale Rousseau of Productions de la tortue qui danse (Dancing Turtle Productions) is passionate about cultivating people's natural creativity in work and life by teaching the practice of mind mapping. Pascale created her Right-Brain Business Plan on pieces of four-inch-by-six-inch photo paper. She appreciated the fact that the smaller size encouraged her to get to the essence of her business. Following her intuition as she put it all together, Pascale arranged the collaged cards into a circle, like a mandala. Seeing the blank center, she remembered that, earlier, she had spontaneously made a drawing on a piece of photo paper. In an aha moment, when she placed that drawing in the middle of the circle as a finishing touch, she felt the satisfaction of all the pieces falling into place. The magical center of her visual plan reminds her that her business is open and creative.

Consultant and teacher Pascale Rousseau placed her Big-Vision Collage cards in a circle to form a mandala, one of her favorite symbols.

If you want to take up space and have something that you can display on a wall or hang up, you can create a mural, a mobile, or a large bulletin board using the different pieces of your plan. Remember, you can mix and match mediums, too. Perhaps you will post the high-level vision artwork in your studio and store all the detailed information, like your financials, completed play sheets, and notes, in a beautifully decoupaged box.

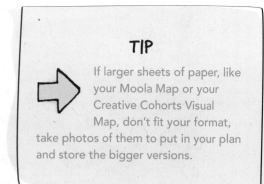

TIP

If larger sheets of paper, like your Moola Map or your Creative Cohorts Visual Map, don't fit your format, take photos of them to put in your plan and store the bigger versions.

There are numerous ways to weave the pieces all together. The only limit is your imagination. Don't get hung up on deciding what the absolutely perfect method is. Focus on finding a fun and accessible format

SUCCESS STORY

As the owner of EndWell Coaching, Kristina Ender empowers clients to discover their passion for living adventurous lives. While weaving together all the pieces of her Right-Brain Business Plan, Kristina discovered areas where her coaching practice and Pilates business intersected. She now uses more movement in her coaching workshops and provides her Pilates clients with more accountability tools. Kristina also identified opportunities for complementary partnerships. She is colaunching a new wellness center that integrates coaching, Pilates, dance, spirituality, and more. When she realized that her strength is helping clients embrace their vision, she partnered up with a fellow coach whose strength is helping clients create systems and processes to make visions real. Together the two coaches are codeveloping programs, retreats, and products.

After seeing all the pieces of her Right-Brain Business Plan together, Kristina created her Hearty Highlights to help set the stage for her visual plan. Originally she thought she would shrink her pages to make a small, portable plan. However, as her big vision came to life more fully, she decided to use the vibrant pages in all their glory. She put her collages, play sheets, and notes into large presentation folders so she could easily display her vision and share it with others. Now isn't that grand?

Coach, workshop leader, and Pilates instructor Kristina Ender of EndWell Coaching combined all the elements of her Right-Brain Business Plan into three large presentation folders. The one shown here includes her Hearty Highlights and her Business Self-Portrait.

that works for you. Package it in a way that inspires you. Your Right-Brain Business Plan can and will evolve, both in its physical form and in the content that graces its pages (or pockets, or petals, or poster board).

EXERCISE

Creating a Helping of Hearty Highlights

Now that you've gone through the entire process, consider creating a Hearty Highlights index card that will serve as your right-brain alternative to the traditional executive summary. Take a look at all the different pieces of your plan, including your big vision and values, your Passion and Purpose Proclamation, your Perfect Customer Portraits, your Business Self-Portrait, and your Getting the Word out and Moola goals. Then write three or four sentences to sum up your plan (using fun, colored markers helps). It might look something like this:

"My business is [business name goes here]. My passion and purpose is to help [a brief description of your perfect customers goes here] to [description of how you help them goes here] by offering my [products and/or services go here]. What makes my business unique is [reference your Business Self-Portrait here]. In the next [year, two years, or five years], my goal is to [highlight some key goals here, including Getting the Word Out and Moola goals]."

EXERCISE

Tailoring Your Plan to Suit the Suits

For many creative entrepreneurs, a business plan is for their eyes only. A vivid, visual version is a perfect fit for their internal strategizing and planning. But if you're gearing up to ask for a bank loan, apply for a grant, or woo investors or potential partners, you'll need a buttoned-down version that speaks your external audience's language. If that's the case, read on.

If not, you can skip ahead to the "Giving Your Finished Plan the Once-Over" section at the end of this chapter. Or feel free to skim through the following "Framework for a More Formal Format" section to see if any other parts of the plan catch your fancy, and make sure to read the Left-Brain Checklist to be certain you've incorporated all the main parts of your Right-Brain Business Plan. While you may not be asking for funding yet, pondering the following questions may help you prepare for taking your business to the next level.

Just as it's probably not a good idea to wear your ripped jeans, skull-and-crossbones hand-knitted sweater, and cool combat boots

RIGHT-BRAIN BOOSTER

Lighten things up by pretending you're writing a high-profile feature article starring you and your fabulous business for your favorite magazine, a top-notch newspaper, or a prestigious industry publication. Use your imagination to get the writing started. You can always go back later and edit and polish it and check the tone.

to a posh black-tie cocktail party (unless you want to be a rebel and get kicked out), your business plan should "dress the part." Don't fret. Under its layers of starched lapels and silk stockings, your plan will still be uniquely you; you'll just be presenting it in a way that will be well received by your audience of suits and ties, who tend to take things seriously. And hey, you do mean business, so you're up for the task.

The great news is, you already have the basic elements of your plan in place. You've done the heavy lifting in a fun, right-brain way. Now it's just a matter of translating your visual plan into a more formal, written plan that bankers, investors, and MBA types are used to. It's the same process, but the final product looks different. While we fun creatives may think the "formal attire" is boring, that it strips our colorful plan of its individualistic character, know that you are merely "tailoring" your plan to a particular audience. That's all. The straitlaced package doesn't overshadow the passion and personality you can exude when you're professionally presenting your case. Plus, you can still be inspired by, and operate your creative business according to, your delightful, heartwarming Right-Brain Business Plan. No suit can take that away from you!

Framework for a More Formal Format

At this point you'll trade in your glue sticks and scissors (at least temporarily) for your word-processing program and perhaps a spreadsheet or two. What follows is a standard framework for a formal business plan to share with a bank or investors. As I mentioned before, you've already done the hard work of exploring, analyzing, creating, and planning. By now you've touched upon most of the major sections of a traditional plan — everything except the operational plan. Since an operational plan describes what you need in order to make your business run smoothly, it's usually necessary only for companies that manufacture products. For that reason, I've addressed it only briefly in this chapter.

A traditional business plan typically includes the sections shown in the illustration below. Each section is written in narrative form and can

be as short as a few paragraphs or as long as a page or two. The text is also accompanied by some key financial spreadsheets, which we'll cover later. You'll summarize the visual elements, completed play sheets, and notes from your right-brain rendition into short paragraphs in a left-brain layout. Prompts and questions are provided here to help you compose the sections.

Executive Summary
(Right-Brain Alter Ego: Hearty Highlights)

Although the executive summary is located at the beginning of your document, it's usually written after everything else, since it sums up the whole business plan. Highlight your key points and objectives in a few captivating paragraphs that entice investors to read on. Reference your Hearty Highlights from earlier in this chapter and consider including the following:

- A brief description of your business
- Your company mission (a.k.a. your Passion and Purpose Proclamation)
- Why your audience should invest in your business; back it up with your big vision, what your growth looks like in dollars and cents, what sets you apart, and what your unique opportunity is
- How much money you're requesting, what you need it for, and how you'll pay it back

Company Overview
(Right-Brain Alter Ego: Business Vision and Values)

For this section, reference the right-brain work you did in chapter 2.

The company overview outlines basic information about your business. Use the following questions to help write up one or two paragraphs.

Artist Elaine Coombs's Right-Brain Business Plan is made up of six collaged panels in her studio. A seventh panel, which she carries on a clipboard, outlines her current goals and actions.

- What business are you in?
- What is your company mission statement?
- What products and/or services does your business offer and at what price points?
- Where are you located?
- What's the history of your company? How long have you been in business?

Competitive Analysis
(Right-Brain Alter Ego: Business Landscape)

For this section, reference the right-brain work you did in chapter 3.

The competitive analysis describes where you fit in the marketplace and identifies your competition, your target market, and what sets you apart from your peers. Take a look at your Business Landscape and Market and Trends play sheets as you answer the following questions:

- What does the industry look like?
- What industry trends and opportunities can your business benefit from?
- What barriers or challenges do you face in this industry?
- What is the size of the total market? What percentage will your business target?
- Who are your competitors?
- What needs are you filling?
- What sets you apart?

Management and Personnel Plan
(Right-Brain Alter Ego: Corralling Your Creative Cohorts)

For this section, reference the right-brain work you did in chapter 6.

The management and personnel plan describes your company's organizational structure. Your business may involve just you, or you may have a whole team of people across the country. Answer the questions that make sense for your situation.

- What is the ownership structure of your business? Are you a sole proprietor, limited liability company, or corporation?
- Are you the owner of the business? What's your background and experience? Why are you the best person to run this business?

LEFT-BRAIN CHILL PILL

LB

If you feel lost in translation because you have to force your colorful visual plan into a straitlaced template, you can always hire a consultant to repackage it for you. You've already laid down the groundwork for all the elements of your plan. Just provide the information you gathered for your right-brain version.

- How are you paid? Are you making enough to pay yourself?
- How much have you personally invested in the business already?
- What is the organizational structure of your business? What are the major functions or roles and responsibilities?
- Do you have a team of employees? How are employees paid? What benefits do employees receive? If you don't have employees now, do you plan on hiring some? If so, when will you hire them and for what roles?
- Do you work with independent contractors? If you aren't working with contractors now, do you plan on outsourcing work to some in the future? If so, when will you outsource and for what type of projects?
- Do you have an advisory board (a.k.a. your inner circle of advisors)? If so, make sure to include their names and bios, as their expertise lends credibility to your organization.

> **TIP**
>
> The typical financial reports that lenders and investors want to see include the profit and loss statement, a cash flow statement, a balance sheet, and perhaps a break-even analysis. Check with your lender for the specific information required, and have your accountant or bookkeeper help you with reports and projections.

Marketing Plan
(Right-Brain Alter Ego: Getting the Word Out)

For this section, reference the right-brain work you did in chapter 4.

The marketing plan outlines how and when you intend to reach your target audience. Take a look at your Perfect Customer Portraits and character sketches, meaningful dialogue messages, and Getting the Word Out plan (including the marketing mediums, messages, and timing) as you answer the following questions:

- Who are your perfect customers? Where are they located?
- What are your marketing goals?
- What marketing mediums will you be using?

Financial Plan
(Right-Brain Alter Ego: Managing the Moola)

For this section, reference the right-brain work you did in chapter 5.

The financial plan describes your company's fiscal picture, including how much you think you'll make and how much you think you'll spend. In this section, you'll need to justify the amount of money you're requesting. The financial plan consists of two parts: a written narrative and a spreadsheet or two that show the numbers (typically, the profit and loss statement and the balance sheet).

The written part can be a few paragraphs that describe the key takeaways from your financial analysis. If you're not comfortable with deciphering a bunch of numbers in the profit and loss statement in order to tell a compelling story, I highly recommend working with a bookkeeper, accountant, or other money-minded person in your inner circle. If you're ready to ask for money, you're ready to have professional help with your numbers.

TIP

Circle back to your financial plan and action plan to see if any additional updates are needed based on new information from the operational plan.

Look at your bank statements, Moola Map, Managing the Moola plan, and Rid the Red, Grow the Green spreadsheet to answer the following questions:

- How much money does your business currently have in cash?
- If you have the information available, what were your actual income and expenses from last year (by month)? This will come from your previous year's profit and loss statement.
- How much do you plan on making in the next year, mapped out by month? How much do you plan on making quarterly in the next three years and the next five years? Use the profit and loss statement to project your income.
- What are your estimated expenses for the next year, three years, and five years? Use the profit and loss statement to project your expenses.

- How much is your business asking for as a loan or as capital? What are the specific things you need the money for (examples: equipment, remodeling a retail space, hiring employees, or launching a marketing campaign)?
- How do you plan to pay the money back?

Operational Plan
(Right-Brain Alter Ego: Smooth Sailing System)

The operational plan describes the logistical and procedural requirements of your work — how the work gets done — and is useful especially if you make or manufacture products. Your right brain can think of this section as your Smooth Sailing System. If you provide a service, you will most likely skip this part. Don't get freaked out by all the questions. Answer only the ones that are relevant to your business.

- What kind of inventory do you need to have on hand, such as raw materials, supplies, samples, or finished goods? How much inventory do you need to purchase, and by when? Where will you store this inventory?
- What companies or individuals do you buy your materials from? Who are your backup suppliers, in case your main supplier goes out of business or a product is out of stock?
- What tools or equipment do you need in order to run your business or produce your goods? Do you rent or own your equipment? What is the process for regular repairs and maintenance? If the core of your business relies on this equipment, what is your contingency plan if something needs to be fixed?

TIP

Don't worry about documenting all the nitty-gritty operational details in your formal business plan. Although it's a good idea to spell out such details in an employee manual, they simply aren't needed in the business plan. Looking for a creative way to include the operational plan in your visual Right-Brain Business Plan? Draw diagrams, create a storyboard, or make a colorful checklist.

- Is there any manufacturing involved in making your goods? Do you produce an original and then reproduce that? Do you make the reproductions yourself, or hire out this job?
- Does anyone else, such as wholesalers or sales agents, a distribution center or a warehouse, distribute your work? How do you communicate with them?
- What are the physical requirements of your workspace or location? Do you need any special insurance coverage or business permits? Do you rent or own?
- What policies and procedures do you have in place for returns, collecting payment, and refunds?

Other Things to Consider

Depending on your situation, you may also want to include additional documentation, such as your marketing materials, pertinent articles about your industry, more detailed financial reports or projections, highlights from your action plan, or any other important information that will help make your case.

Giving Your Finished Plan the Once-Over

Whether you've completed the full-blown, formal, left-brain plan or you've put the finishing touches on your creative, visual, right-brain version, make sure you give your finished plan the once-over. Have you touched on all the important pieces? Review the Left-Brain Checklist at the end of this chapter to help you cross your t's and dot your i's.

Bring other people, like your inner circle of advisors or other creative cohorts, back into the picture to ask what might be missing. By asking questions, testing your assumptions, and giving feedback, your collaborators will help you avoid blind spots. You may even find more ways to spruce up your plan.

Florist Nicole Mason arranged pieces of her Right-Brain Business Plan in an accordion book decorated with paper petals, collages, fun embellishments, and colorful cards listing her left-brain details.

As you've probably experienced by now, creating your business plan is an ever-evolving, nonlinear process. Many of the sections are linked. For example, some of the marketing mediums you chose in chapter 4 may require outside help and cost money. That means you'll need to circle back to your Creative Cohorts Visual Map to note a contractor need, and return to the Moola Map or Rid the Red, Grow the Green spreadsheet to make sure additional expenses are included. By giving your plan the once-over, you'll see how everything ties together.

I hope that, as you take time to look at your plan as a whole, you also acknowledge the amazing vision you've put out in the world. While the planning process may have been overwhelming at times, by sticking with it and developing your plan little by little, you've painted a vibrant and exciting picture of where you want to take your business. In the next chapter, you'll explore how to maintain the magic and momentum of your brilliant vision.

- Integrate all the pieces into your visual Right-Brain Business Plan.
- Create your Hearty Highlights to sum up your entire plan.
- Tailor your visual plan to suit the suits (if a more formal plan is needed).

LEFT-BRAIN CHECKLIST

Before moving on to the final chapter, review the checklist below. Your left brain will thank you!

- ❏ I have articulated my business vision and values.
- ❏ I have defined my mission statement (that is, Passion and Purpose Proclamation).
- ❏ I know where I stand in the business landscape: how I'm leveraging industry trends, who my competitors are, what my market is, and what my challenges and opportunities are.
- ❏ I know who my perfect customers are.
- ❏ I have a marketing plan to reach my perfect customers.
- ❏ I know my numbers, including my projected income, expenses, and profits.
- ❏ I have my team and support structure in place, and roles and responsibilities are clearly defined.
- ❏ I have mapped out goals, strategies, and action steps to support my business plan.
- ❏ I have a visual plan that inspires me.
- ❏ I have a written, narrative business plan that has been reviewed by my inner circle of advisors and is ready to take to investors (if this applies to you).

Maintaining the Magic and Momentum

Keep Your Right-Brain Business Plan Alive

Bravo to you for making it through the creative exploration and planning process (and even bearing with me on some of those left-brain details)! Creating, exploring, and planning are just part of the fun. The other exciting part is growing your business and truly making your vision real. You've done a great job of crafting an inspiring, visual plan for your business success. Now how will you maintain the magic and momentum?

This final chapter offers you lighthearted and practical pointers for keeping your Right-Brain Business Plan alive. We'll talk about ways to stay connected to your vision. You'll come face-to-face with your inner critic so you can bust right through the doubt and keep moving forward. You'll learn how to conduct regular check-ins to assess your progress, how right-brain thinking can continue to be your ally, and how to celebrate your successes. And lastly, you'll discover ways to connect with other creative entrepreneurs for more support and inspiration, and I'll suggest possible next steps you can take to continue growing your business.

As you continue on your entrepreneurial journey, here are some reminders to spark your creative process. A few of them recap important principles already covered in this book, and others are simple ways to keep the magic alive.

Stay connected to your vision. Keep your Right-Brain Business Plan in plain sight. Display it on your desk. Carry it with you in your bag. Let it be an inspirational, tangible reminder to connect with the big vision of your business and the steps that will help you make that vision come true.

For daily inspiration, post your plan near your workspace — just as Micheline Courtemanche of Betty and Bing, a letterpress studio, did with her Big-Vision Collage, master calendar, Perfect Customer Portraits, and Moola Map.

Add to your Right-Brain Business Plan. Your visual plan is a living, breathing work of art that gets to evolve right alongside your creative business. As you gather new inspiration and new ideas, capture them on your plan, paste new images onto your Big-Vision Collage, and include new cards for your perfect customers, offerings, or anything else you gain new insights about. As you learn more about your business and where you want it to go, make sure your plan reflects that.

Share your Right-Brain Business Plan. By sharing your plan and telling others where you want to go, you'll receive help along the way, and you'll help hold yourself accountable for your commitments. Think about which friends, family members, colleagues, and mentors you want to invite into the big picture. No need to bare your heart and soul to your cranky coworker who finds something wrong with everything, or your Uncle Bob who just doesn't get what you do for a living. Pick positive, supportive people who can contribute encouragement, good advice, and constructive feedback. Who will you share your plan with today? And, I bet, as an added good-karma bonus you'll inspire them to move forward with their creative visions, too.

RIGHT-BRAIN BOOSTER

Keep a "kudos and feel-good folder." Collect all the affirming and encouraging emails, cards, and messages you get from your clients, creative cohorts, family, and friends. If you need a positive pick-me-up, read their kind words and remind yourself just how amazing you are.

Enlist professional guidance. If you want individualized, one-on-one support, consider hiring a coach or a consultant to help you take your creative business to the next level. Having a sounding board, impartial feedback, an experienced outside perspective, and accountability can accelerate your progress big time.

Follow the flow. If you're feeling stuck, do something creative to find your flow again. Maybe you could sing a song or knit a scarf. The important thing is that you keep your creative momentum. See what fresh perspective emerges. Read through the "Exercising Your Right-Brain Genius" section later in this chapter for more flow-following fun.

Learn something new. What new thing do you want to know more about in relation to your business? Find fun ways to pick up that knowledge. If you enjoy reading, get an interesting book about your business that speaks to you. If you love interaction, take a class. The more you know, the more empowered you'll feel.

Make time for reflection. At least once every quarter, carve out time to look at where you've been and where you're going. Revisit your plan and update it with new information. Identify where you might need to adjust your course, and acknowledge your successes and accomplishments. Later on in this chapter you'll learn some ways to conduct quarterly check-ins.

Ask for help. Remember, you don't need to do it all. Outsource what you're not as good at or don't enjoy. Delegating frees you up to focus on the heart of your business.

Connect with creative cohorts. Get inspired by other entrepreneurs, kindred spirits, and movers and shakers. Reach out to someone you admire and ask for some mentoring. Make a date with your fellow creative cohorts to brainstorm ideas, play with your Right-Brain Business Plans, and support one another. Together you can help one another grow your businesses. Set up a nurture huddle or find an accountability buddy. Meet regularly to update each other on your progress.

Celebrate your successes. Make sure you acknowledge all the goals you've already achieved. Getting to your big vision is the sum of all the tiny steps you take along the way, so make sure you give yourself credit where credit is due. At the end of this chapter, I'll share more ideas about ways to honor your achievements big and small.

EXERCISE

Getting to Know Your Inner Critic

Name your inner critic. Write a short bio, including a description of what it looks like, its habits and talents, and what it usually says.

My inner critic's name is: _____.

My inner critic's habits and special talents are: _____

_____.

My inner critic is known for saying the following things to me:

_____.

Or write a character sketch of your inner critic, complete with its skills and background story. Or draw, sketch, doodle, paint a picture of, or make a mask of your inner critic. How big is it, what color is it, what does it wear?

As you become better at recognizing when your inner critic is running the show, it becomes much easier to tell it to bug off! When you hear those familiar negative phrases, simply notice that your inner critic has been triggered, show appreciation for its concern, and remind it that you've got lots of support and resources to lean on, and that you'll be just fine. Other inner-critic-busting strategies include taking small steps until you acclimate to the change, asking for support from friends, and reaching into your "kudos and feel-good folder" for a dose of warm fuzzies.

What other strategies could you use to bypass your inner critic?

As mentioned earlier in this chapter, you should, at least every three months, track how well you're doing and make sure you're on your way to reaching the big vision for your business. By reviewing your progress regularly, you'll know when to celebrate your successes, and you'll identify places where you may need to make changes. You can do the check-in by yourself, or you can invite your inner circle of advisors to offer different perspectives. If you gather your inner circle, make sure you send them any pertinent materials ahead of time and are clear about what you want from them in the meeting. Perhaps you'd like them to bring new ideas to the table or review some questions beforehand and be ready for a group discussion. Or you could even hold a virtual meeting by simply sending out a survey or holding a conference call.

Have your Right-Brain Business Plan and all the accoutrements — like your business landscape, Getting the Word Out plan, Managing the Moola plan, and action plan — with you, along with any other relevant up-to-date information, like your sales numbers, client feedback, or website statistics, so you can assess progress.

EXERCISE

Stop, Start, Continue

Begin by doing a simple "stop, start, continue" assessment to identify what's working and what's not. Get out your pink, green, and yellow sticky notes and jot down your thoughts on individual notes, using the color-coding below. If you're in a group, have participants write their answers on separate sticky notes. You can stick all the sticky notes on a flip chart by category and see what themes emerge.

- Stop (pink): What are three to five things that you need to stop doing in your business?

- Start (green): What are three to five things that you need to start doing in your business?
- Continue (yellow): What are three to five things that are working well and that you want to continue?

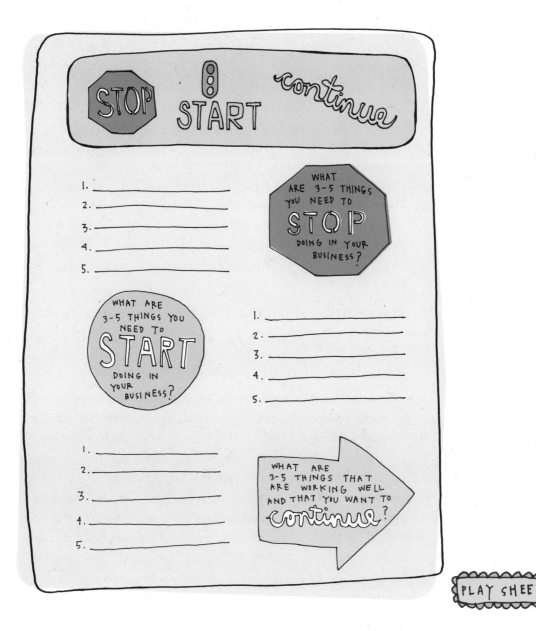

Based on the results, what do you commit to doing or not doing in your business? What resources or support might you need to make that happen?

Take your check-in a step further by asking yourself specific questions, such as the following:

- What new opportunities are available? How are they aligned to my values and vision? Which ones will I incorporate into my plan?
- Are my moola goals on-target? If not, why not? Does my goal or my approach to achieving the goal need to change?
- Are my Getting the Word Out goals on-target? If not, why not? Does my goal or my approach to achieving the goal need to change?
- What new or different approaches to my own business have I learned from my peers and/or the evolving business landscape?
- Does my Right-Brain Business Plan still inspire me? If not, how can I breathe new life into it?
- Am I engaged, having fun, and experiencing joy in my business? If not, what do I need to do differently?

When you're done with your assessment, create an action plan to address the results.

Quarterly Goals Play Sheet

If you like having a one-sheet view of your goals and tasks, then you might want to play with the Quarterly Goals play sheet (download it at Rightbrainbusinessplan.com). Fill in your goals for each quarter on the top row. In the boxes for the months, list the actions you'll take to achieve each goal, including exact dates by which you'll take them. You can also include key events or milestones that you don't want to lose sight of. This gives a nice month-to-month snapshot of where you're headed and how you'll get there. Hang the play sheet on a bulletin board or someplace else where you can view it regularly. Or tuck it into a pocket in your Right-Brain Business Plan. Make sure to revisit your goals during your quarterly check-in. Allow the OCD part of you to check everything off once you've accomplished it.

QUARTERLY GOALS

QUARTER 1	QUARTER 2	QUARTER 3	QUARTER 4
GOALS:	GOALS:	GOALS:	GOALS:
January	April	July	October
February	May	August	November
March	June	September	December

PLAY SHEET

Letter Lessons in Manifestation: The Three P's and a D

When you've laid out a grand big picture for your creative business, it can sometimes feel daunting or unattainable because it is huge and exciting. Part of maintaining the magic and momentum is to stay connected to your inspiring dream even when you might be doubtful or discouraged.

Here are some lessons I've learned when it comes to manifesting big visions.

Patience. When I created my first Right-Brain Business Plan and wrote a letter from the future to myself, I was bursting at the seams, ready to have it all start coming true immediately. While some milestones happened for me on schedule or even faster than anticipated, the majority of them took time. Lots and lots of time. Sometimes the bigger vision has to be delayed because smaller pieces of the puzzle must fall into place first. You may not even be aware of these smaller pieces lining up to get you to where you need to go. Knitters know that it can take a while for the pattern to emerge. You need to give your vision time to take shape and gain momentum.

RIGHT-BRAIN BOOSTER

Track your progress (with flair, of course). When you're juggling many creative projects (as most nonlinear right-brainers do), it can feel like you're not getting anything done. Rather than get frustrated, acknowledge that you're moving forward, even if it's one baby step at a time. A satisfying way to do this is to find a beautiful bowl, and each time you complete something from any of your projects, drop a bead into the bowl. Before you know it, your bowl will runneth over.

Persistence. Thinking that the vision will progress in a specific sequence can lead to frustration when things don't go as planned. Believe me, I know! However, by staying with it, you will start to see connections between various parts of your vision. So, forge ahead while holding your intention lightly. You'll be open to synchronicity and surprised by what unfolds.

Presence. People won't know about you if you don't show up. So have a physical presence. Build a website, set up an Etsy store, post flyers for your workshop, go to an event and meet new people, dialogue on Twitter, have a booth at a show. In chapter 4, we covered a lot of practical ways for you to get yourself out there.

Showing up also means being fully present in the moment. When you're present, you engage with people in an authentic and meaningful way. Ultimately, it's you, not your marketing materials, who will enroll your perfect customers.

Drishti (or point of view, if you prefer a fourth P). Loosely translated from Sanskrit, *drishti* can mean "vision," "insight," or "point of view." In a yoga pose, *drishti* helps you practice your internal and external focus by holding your gaze at a particular spot. *Drishti* allows you to simultaneously look inward as you connect with your highest self, and outward as you set your attention consciously in the physical world.

The key to *drishti* is holding a soft focus. You don't need to bore a hole in the wall with a hard, laserlike stare. If you do have an extreme case of tunnel vision, you'll certainly miss out on a lot of other important aspects of your experience. Just as you don't need to crane your neck in a seated forward bend to see your big toe, you don't need to fixate or tie yourself up in knots to force your Right-Brain Business Plan to manifest. Don't strain yourself to reach your goals. As you take this lesson away from the yoga mat, remember to hold your vision lightly. Oh, and breathe!

Have a Life

Speaking of yoga, I would be remiss if I didn't mention that sometimes the demands of entrepreneurship will throw you off balance. It isn't worth sacrificing a rich and fulfilling life just to have a successful, creative business. Who cares that you're rolling in dough if you don't have time to enjoy yourself, spend time with your loved ones, or take pleasure in the creative pastimes that used to bring a smile to your face? Might as well go right back to your cubicle-land job!

As you do in your business quarterly check-ins, make sure you check in with yourself regularly — not just regarding your work, but also concerning the other important facets of your life, like health and well-being, personal growth, relationships, physical space, and fun. How would you rate each of these facets of your life on a scale of one through ten, with ten being "totally satisfied"? If some of your scores are low, what actions can you take to move the needle up?

Balancing Both Brains

Another important way to find balance as a creative entrepreneur is to let your thought processes flow freely between your right brain and left brain. As you've seen throughout this book, each side of your noggin offers valuable gifts. It's a matter of knowing when to lean on which hemisphere for what and, many times, seamlessly integrating the two.

The Left-Brain/Right-Brain play sheets on pages 196 and 197 will help you assess how well you're accessing both sides in the planning process. Color in the number of hearts and stars to show to what level you agree with the statements. Filling in all five means you completely agree; leaving them blank means you completely disagree.

How does this right-brain/left-brain assessment differ from your initial responses to two questions in the introduction to this book: "Which description do you feel more comfortable with, and identify with, and why? Does your preference differ according to the circumstances?" And how has making your right brain your business buddy helped you to tackle the left-brain details that may have once seemed daunting?

Exercising Your Right-Brain Genius

As we talked about in the beginning of this book, your right brain is a gift in your creative business. It plays an important part in helping you kick off your business planning in a fun, big-picture way. It also plays a vital role in helping you maintain the magic and momentum along your entrepreneurial journey. It's what will keep your work fun, engaging, and meaningful for you, even when times are tough.

Below are some suggested practices to help you continue making friends with your right brain:

- Move your body. Dance, do yoga, walk the dog, run a marathon, stretch.
- Enliven your senses. Experience colors, images, smells, sounds, tastes, and textures.
- Look for a metaphor to describe your situation.
- Scribble with your nondominant hand.
- Sing a silly song. Exercise your voice aloud.
- Invite randomness into your life. Embrace nonlinear and intuitive approaches.
- Connect with people, build relationships, and foster community.
- Tell a story. Tell your business as a story.
- Search for the deeper meaning.
- Laugh at a good joke. Laugh at yourself. Laugh until you cry.
- Make something with your hands.
- Go on a play date with yourself or with friends. Do something that brings you joy or unleashes your inner child.
- Practice meditation. Breathe deeply. Slow down to stay present in your life and in your work.
- Spend some time in nature or wide-open spaces. Allow yourself to feel like you're a part of something greater than yourself.

All these simple suggestions can help you breathe new life into your business and your creativity. Pick a few to play with this week. Think of them as enchanting toys in your creative entrepreneurship's toy chest. Pull one out when you need to shake things up, when you want a fresh perspective, or when you simply need a right-brain break from some left-brain drudgery. See what brings a smile to your face and a spring to your step.

While these activities may not necessarily seem like work, trust that by giving yourself a playful space you're enhancing your overall ability to show up fully on the job and at home. You may even develop some of these as ongoing practices to help you engage regularly with your right brain. Weave them into the fabric of your work and personal life and see how effective and enlivening this integration can be.

LEFT BRAIN

the mind + matter meter

I have a plan of action.

☆ ☆ ☆ ☆ ☆

I know my numbers.

☆ ☆ ☆ ☆ ☆

I have information and "data" to help
me track my progress.

☆ ☆ ☆ ☆ ☆

I've asked myself the tough questions.

☆ ☆ ☆ ☆ ☆

I'm taking action in the real world,
not just living in my imagination.

☆ ☆ ☆ ☆ ☆

PLAY SHEET

Right brain

the heart + soul meter

I find meaning in my work.

I'm emotionally connected to my work
& am excited & passionate about what I do.

My business is aligned with my values.

My business allows me to express my
creative vision.

I'm connecting with other people in a
meaningful way.

Being a creative entrepreneur takes guts, backbone, heart, and soul. You're continually on the go, facing challenges, and seizing opportunities, so it's important to find time to celebrate wherever you are on your entrepreneurial journey. Otherwise you'll burn yourself out, and you won't have any idea how far you've come. Plus, it's just more fun when you kick up your heels from time to time.

Whether you've just landed your biggest client yet, sold your first product (hey, selling to your mom counts!), or tackled a pesky item on your action plan, every step forward is something to celebrate. Even celebrating the steps backward, the failures, and disappointments can be valuable, too. While they may not seem as pleasant, they're chock-full of valuable learning, and that is really worth honoring.

? RIGHT-BRAIN REFLECTION

Take a few moments to reflect on the following questions:

- What are at least three things, big or small, that you can acknowledge about your progress right now?
- What are you most proud of?
- What have you learned about yourself through your business?

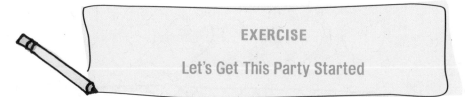

EXERCISE

Let's Get This Party Started

Think of ways you like to celebrate, from the extravagant to the mundane. They don't have to be time-consuming or expensive (or they absolutely can be; it's up to you!). Perhaps you enjoy a nice cup of tea after sending out your monthly newsletter, or you reward yourself with a rocking night on the town with your friends after wrapping up a large project. Some of my favorite celebratory acts include pampering myself with an hour-long massage (sometimes an hour and a half, if I deserve extra kudos), sitting outside and enjoying the sunshine, or going out to a fancy dinner with my hubby. Just connect with what brings you joy.

Identify a list of at least five to ten ways you like to celebrate.

Find ways to celebrate the three things you acknowledged yourself for in the reflection above.

Make it a goal to celebrate something at least once a week for the next month. Choose a significant milestone that you want to honor when you've reached it.

Build in celebration time after each of your quarterly check-ins.

If you're really willing to put yourself out there, pick a date to throw yourself a big party to celebrate your accomplishment. Send invitations to your friends and creative cohorts so you have something to aim toward. It will serve as a great milestone, and it always helps to celebrate the people who have supported you on your journey.

LEFT-BRAIN CHILL PILL

If you're ever feeling superstuck or down in the dumps, find one itty-bitty thing you can celebrate, and celebrate now! I don't care if it's the fact that you just replenished the staples in your stapler. When you're feeling low, every little step forward counts. Being a creative entrepreneur can be a tough job, so cut yourself some slack.

Creating Community and Connection

Connecting with a community of kindred spirits is a powerful and inspiring way to keep your momentum going. My business really started to take off when I put myself out there, both in person and online. Sure, it was a stretch for this homebody introvert, but I participated in (and even led) a local women's entrepreneurial group, networked with fellow coaches and artists, and built incredible friendships through the virtual community of creative bloggers. I know that these valuable relationships have had a huge impact on my business on numerous levels. I learn loads from my peers; I receive invaluable support, feedback, and encouragement; I'm constantly inspired by hearing what my fellow creative cohorts are up to in this world, and so much more. I invite you to reach out in ways that feel authentic to you.

You can start by posting photos of your Right-Brain Business Plan on your blog or Flickr.com, or cavort with a community of other creative entrepreneurs at Rightbrainbusinessplan.com. See what other right-brainers are doing in their creative businesses and engage in dialogue. Visit a local networking meeting and see if you can pick out some of your peeps. Check out the Resources section at the back of this book for other suggested creative-entrepreneur groups and online communities. Your right brain craves connection, so honor your need for relationships in a way that feels good to you.

Where to Go from Here

Your Right-Brain Business Plan serves as a source of magical inspiration that keeps you connected to your vision and on track to make it come alive. In this book, you've learned a creative process that you can use again and again as you grow and refine your business, whether you explore additional products and services or even launch a new business. Your Right-Brain Business Plan has helped build your solid foundation and framed your creative mind-set.

As you expand to the next level, you may require some additional and specific expertise or support. For example, maybe after a year spent getting your art business off the ground, you're ready to move from your kitchen to a full-fledged studio. After revisiting your business landscape and making a Moola Map for this new goal, you realize you'll need to ask for a loan to get your ideal space. You might also need to draw up a lease contract with the help of a real estate attorney and purchase special insurance to protect yourself and your business. Whatever unique turns your creative business takes, trust that you have the know-how, connections, and confidence to take the next step. You've laid the important groundwork that will allow your business to keep flourishing. Continue to let your right brain dream big, and trust that your left brain (with inspiration from its creative counterpart, of course) will help you access the resources you need to make it happen.

Throughout this process, you've probably also discovered that the more you know about yourself, the more you can authentically integrate all of yourself into your work. Personal growth means business growth. And business growth means personal growth. Entrepreneurship is a constant learning process and a journey of self-discovery. Enjoy the ride.

And That's a Wrap

While this is the end of the book, it's also only the beginning. As a right-brain entrepreneur, you're pioneering a new way of working in the world that values your creative gifts. Live passionately. Display your Right-Brain Business Plan proudly. Celebrate your intuitive genius. And remember, this is not business as usual!

Glossary

A Right-Brain Take on Common Left-Brain Business Terms

Traditional business language can sound masculine, even warlike. So, for connoisseurs of a more right-brain, feminine approach, I've translated some of the bland, conventional business concepts into tastier terms.

TRADITIONAL LEFT-BRAIN BUSINESS TERM	CREATIVE RIGHT-BRAIN ALTER EGO	DEFINITION
Board of advisors	Inner circle of advisors	Experts and advisors who give you guidance, support, and feedback
Competition	Colleagues or peers	Fellow entrepreneurs in the same field and businesses similar to yours; people to learn from and potentially partner with
Competitive analysis	Business Landscape	Describes where you fit in the marketplace, how you stand out from others in similar businesses, and where your opportunities are
Elevator speech/pitch	Engaging in a meaningful dialogue	A concise and personable way of describing your business
Executive summary	Hearty Highlights	A brief overview of your entire business plan

Continued

TRADITIONAL LEFT-BRAIN BUSINESS TERM	CREATIVE RIGHT-BRAIN ALTER EGO	DEFINITION
Financial plan	Moola Map, Moola goals	How much money you need to make, how much you'll spend, and how you'll make money
Management team, personnel, organizational structure	Creative Cohorts Visual Map	A visual of the people who support you and your business and who help get the work done
Marketing	Getting the Word Out	An enticing invitation to connect with your perfect customers
Mastermind or accountability group	Nurture huddle	A safe, collaborative gathering of peers who mutually encourage and inspire one another
Mission statement	Passion and Purpose Proclamation	A short description of what has heart and meaning for you and your perfect customers, and how you're making a positive impact through your work
Operational plan	Smooth Sailing System	How the work gets done via your business processes, policies, and procedures, especially if you manufacture products
Target audience demographics/segments	Your perfect customers	The people most likely to buy your products or services
Work sheet	Play sheet	A fun, visual form or map for exploring an idea or depicting information

Resources

’ve recommended some reading and resources to help you on your entrepreneurial journey. Visit Rightbrainbusinessplan.com for more suggested resources and links.

Creative Business

Craft, Inc.: Business Planner, by Meg Mateo Ilasco.
Craft, Inc.: Turn Your Creative Hobby into a Business, by Meg Mateo Ilasco.
The Creative Entrepreneur: A DIY Visual Guidebook for Making Business Ideas Real, by Lisa Sonora Beam.
Tranquilista: Mastering the Art of Enlightened Work and Mindful Play, by Kimberly Wilson.

Right-Brain Inspiration

The Back of the Napkin: Solving Problems and Selling Ideas with Pictures, by Dan Roam.
Creative Visualization: Use the Power of Your Imagination to Create What You Want in Your Life, by Shakti Gawain.
My Stroke of Insight: A Brain Scientist's Personal Journey, by Dr. Jill Bolte Taylor.
Stimulated!: Habits to Spark Your Creative Genius at Work, by Andrew Pek and Jeannine McGlade.
Visual Thinking: Tools for Mapping Your Ideas, by Nancy Margulies and Christine Valenza.
A Whole New Mind: Why Right-Brainers Will Rule the Future, by Daniel Pink.

Business Wisdom

Sacred Commerce: Business as a Path of Awakening, by Matthew Engelhart and Terces Engelhart.

Visionary Business: An Entrepreneur's Guide to Success, by Marc Allen.

Painting Your Business Landscape

To find out more about yourself for your Business Self-Portrait, send an online survey to your customers or friends and family using www.surveymonkey.com.

Getting the Word Out with Marketing

Attracting Perfect Customers: The Power of Strategic Synchronicity, by Stacey Hall and Jan Brogniez.

Guerrilla Marketing: Easy and Inexpensive Strategies for Making Big Profits from Your Small Business, by Jay Conrad Levinson.

Karma Queens, Geek Gods, and Innerpreneurs: Meet the 9 Consumer Types Shaping Today's Marketplace, by Ron Rentel and Joe Zellnik.

POP! Create the Perfect Pitch, Title, and Tagline for Anything, by Sam Horn.

To subscribe to a free PR inquiry listing service, visit Help a Reporter Out at www.helpareporter.com.

Managing the Moola

The Accounting Game: Basic Accounting Fresh from the Lemonade Stand, by Darrell Mullis and Judith Orloff.

How to Read a Financial Report: Wringing Vital Signs out of the Numbers, by John A. Tracy.

Money Magic: Unleashing Your True Potential for Prosperity and Fulfillment, by Deborah L. Price.

Corralling Your Creative Cohorts

Never Eat Alone: And Other Secrets to Success, One Relationship at a Time, by Keith Ferrazzi.

Work the Pond!: Use the Power of Positive Networking to Leap Forward in Work and Life, by Darcy Rezac.

For setting up a free conference call number for your nurture huddle or inner circle of advisors, try www.freeconferencecalling.com, www.nocostconference.com, or www.freeconferencecall.com.

For finding outside services or temporary help, search sites such as
www.resourcenation.com/business or www.elance.com.

For finding a coach, visit the International Coach Federation,
www.coachfederation.org; or the Coaches Training Institute,
www.thecoaches.com.

For social media, check out: www.twitter.com, www.facebook.com,
www.ning.com, or www.linkedin.com.

For networking online and in person, visit www.meetup.com,
www.ladieswholaunch.com, www.savorthesuccess.com,
www.hatchnetwork.com, www.bni.com, or www.ewomennetwork.com.

Action Planning

One Small Step Can Change Your Life: The Kaizen Way, by Robert Maurer.

Tailoring Your Plan to Suit the Suits

Business Plan Pro is a business planning software program that has
detailed templates and a wide variety of sample business plans. See
www.businessplanpro.com.

The One-Day Marketing Plan: Organizing and Completing a Plan That Works, by
Roman Hiebing and Scott Cooper.

The One Page Business Plan for the Creative Entrepreneur, by James T. Horan Jr.

The Successful Business Plan, Secrets and Strategies 4th edition, by Rhonda
Abrams.

*Your First Business Plan, A Simple Question-and-Answer Format Designed to Help
You Write Your Own Plan 5th edition*, by Brian Hazelgren.

Art Supplies

Blick Art, for general art supplies. Online store and locations across the United
States; www.dickblick.com.

Levenger, for Circa notebooks. Online store and select retail locations across the
United States; www.levenger.com.

Michael's, for general arts and crafts supplies. Retail locations across the United
States and Canada; www.michaels.com.

Paper Source, for accordion book kits, paper, envelopes, and cards. Online store
and locations across the United States; www.paper-source.com.

Featured Right-Brain Entrepreneurs

Tracey Asai
Tracey Asai Designs
www.traceyasaidesigns.com

Rebecca Badger
Rebecca Badger Marketing
www.workwithrebecca.com

Julie Benjamin
Little Lane Studios
www.littlelanestudios.com

Lauren Brownstein
Pitch Consulting, LLC
www.pitchconsulting.com

Michelle Casey
Collage Your World
www.collageyourworld.com

Violette Clark
Violette's Creative Juice
www.violette.ca

Elaine Coombs
Elaine Coombs Fine Art
www.elainecoombs.com

Micheline Courtemanche
Betty and Bing Letterpress
www.bettyandbing.com

Amy A. Crawley
Moonroom Crafts
Amy A. Crawley Fine Art
www.AmyACrawley.com

Tori Deaux
The Circus Serene
www.circusserene.com

Tanya Demello
My Little Life
www.doc-you-mentation.blogspot.com

Beth DeZiel
Professional organizer and concierge
www.bethdeziel.com

Amy Egenberger
Spirit Out!, Inc.
www.amyegenberger.com

Kristina Ender
EndWell Coaching
www.endwellcoaching.com

Danielle David Grinnen
Deliante Designs, LLC
www.deliantedesigns.com

Mary Daniel Hobson
www.marydanielhobson.com

Nicole Mason
Floral designer

Ana Ottman
Red Dress Studios
www.reddressstudios.com

Bevla Reeves
HairConspiracy.com
www.hairconspiracy.com

Pascale Rousseau
Productions de la tortue qui danse
www.productionsdelatortuequidanse.com

Earleen Stanwaity
Ethereal Enterprises, LLC
www.etherealspirit.com

Rena Tucker
U.S.A. Mercantile Corp.
www.usamercantilecorp.com

Acknowledgments

I'm extremely grateful to the countless creative cohorts who helped make this book possible. In particular, I'd like to thank:

My husband and soul mate, Brian Ng, for his loving support and encouragement, for helping me edit my manuscript, and for handling so many behind-the-scenes details, including photographing much of the featured artwork and being my left-brain tech guru.

My book coach, Jan King, for guiding me through the publishing process with her endless patience, wise insights, and heartfelt support.

My editor, Georgia Hughes, and her wonderful team at New World Library for championing this book and being an absolute pleasure to work with.

My ultimate creative cohort, fabulous friend, and talented designer, Kate Prentiss, for helping me bring my creative visions to life and for doing the darling illustrations that grace these pages.

My awesome nurture huddlers, with a special shout-out to Leah Piken Kolidas and Jessie Marianiello for providing extra boosts of nurturing and huddling.

My draft manuscript rock-star reviewers, Britt Bravo, Linda Kennedy, Leah Piken Kolidas, Kristen Morse, Jamie Ridler, and Starla Sireno, for their generous feedback and valuable insights about enhancing this book.

My virtual assistant, Lisa Jacobson, for taking care of my many to-dos with positivity and professionalism.

My fellow New World Library author Kimberly Wilson, for inspiring and supporting me and for generously sharing lessons learned from her publishing journey.

My intuitive painting teacher, Chris Zydel, who magically appeared in my life at the time I was making the goal of this book real, and who helped me paint through the ups and downs of the writing process.

My bookkeeper, Ana Duffy, for doing a sanity check on many of the numbers in this book.

All the featured right-brain entrepreneurs in this book, for kindly sharing their creative visions and wonderful artwork.

All my other creative cohorts and friends, especially Julie Tsai and Amy Siu, for cheering me on.

All my mentors, teachers, clients, course participants, blog readers, and fellow right-brain entrepreneurs, whom I learn from every day.

My parents, for their lifelong support of my creative endeavors and for showing me how creativity can be part of daily life. My mom, Irene Lee, ever since I can remember, has always had a crafty project at hand, from doll-making to knitting to making me a matching Strawberry Shortcake dress and cake for my seventh birthday. My dad, Curtis Lee, after retiring from a long, very left-brain career as an engineer, pursued his culinary passions and makes the most delicious pasta dishes and desserts.

Index

About the Author

Right-brain entrepreneur Jennifer Lee is a certified coach, writer, artist, and yogini and the founder of Artizen Coaching. Before pursuing her own passions full-time, she consulted for ten years for companies such as Gap Inc., Accenture, Sony, and HP, helping leaders and organizations manage change. As a director of executive development for Gap Inc., she led onboarding and coaching programs for those at the level of vice president and up. She grew her private coaching business in her spare time, and in 2006 Jennifer made the leap from corporate America to entrepreneurship after realizing she needed to stop living her own dream on the side.

Now she is on a mission to empower people to awaken their innate creativity and make a living doing what they love. When she's not coaching, writing, or leading groups, she's either painting up a storm, reading in her hammock, practicing yoga, making arts and crafts, or indulging in a midday nap (one of the fabulous perks of being self-employed).

Jennifer holds a bachelor's degree in communication studies from UCLA and a master's degree in communication management from USC. She lives in the San Francisco Bay Area with her creative, rather left-brain husband and their adorable beagle mix.

For creative inspiration and more information on Jennifer's coaching, workshops, e-courses, and innovative products, visit her websites:

Artizencoaching.com and *Rightbrainbusinessplan.com*